"Steve Sampson hits the bull's-eye in his new and revised book on the Jezebel spirit. Almost every page gives insight into the problems we often confront relating to others throughout our lives. This book is essential for every married couple and every pastor as a manual for counsel, wisdom and victory. True stories give insight into the human psyche as Steve spells out the subtle but powerful ways in which the power of this dark spiritual force tries to control and bind us, whether we are male or female. Just as Elijah overcame the sorcerers on Mount Carmel, you will learn to discern and defeat this illegitimate, tormenting spirit. Thank you, Steve, for a powerful treatise on setting the captives free in this strategic hour."

Mahesh Chavda, senior pastor, All Nations Church

"When I read a book I want to know who the author is and whether or not he is trustworthy. Steve Sampson, a unique minister of truth and Spirit inspiration, is a chosen vessel of God who has proven his trust, faith and love to millions of believing Christians, Bible scholars, pastors and teachers. I TRUST HIM.

"As you read this book, written from Steve's heart, know that his chief motivation is to help you live a happy and fulfilled life in a world teeming with deceit and lies. He dares to expose the Jezebel spirit wherever it lurks and gives direction how to live in a dying world. There seem to be some Jezebels everywhere you go, in the hidden rooms of our political society, the corners of the church sanctuary or in the secret alleys of our minds. This book, pointing out the evils of the Jezebel spirit—past, present and future—is rich with little-known facts and subtleties. Read, meditate and act!"

Dr. R. L. Cornwall, co-author, *The Five Foundations of Marriage*; pastor for sixty years

"*Confronting Jezebel* is marvelously written, biblically based and easy to understand. This book is filled with truth and examples that will equip every believer on how to spot and deal with Jezebel. The keys provided will result in victoriously defeating and overcoming this spirit. I recommend this book to be part of your library."

Dr. Ché Ahn, senior pastor, HROCK Church, Pasadena, California; president, Harvest International Ministry; international chancellor, Wagner Leadership Institute

Other Books by Steve Sampson

Breaking the Bondage Barrier . . . Taking the Limits off God

Discerning and Defeating the Ahab Spirit: The Key to Breaking Free From Jezebel

Don't Talk to Me Now, Lord . . . I'm Trying to Pray

Those Who Expect Nothing Are Never Disappointed

You Can Hear the Voice of God

You Can't Use Me Today, Lord . . . I Don't Feel Spiritual

REVISED AND EXPANDED EDITION

CONFRONTING
JEZEBEL

DISCERNING AND DEFEATING THE
SPIRIT OF CONTROL

Steve Sampson

Chosen
a division of Baker Publishing Group
Minneapolis, Minnesota

Published by Chosen Books
11400 Hampshire Avenue South
Bloomington, Minnesota 55438
www.chosenbooks.com

Chosen Books is a division of
Baker Publishing Group, Grand Rapids, Michigan

Printed in the United States of America

Library of Congress Cataloging-in-Publication Data
Sampson, Steve, 1948–
    Confronting Jezebel : discerning and defeating the spirit of control / Steve Sampson. — Rev. and expanded ed.
        p.   cm.
    ISBN 978-0-8007-9475-0 (pbk.)
    1. Control (Psychology)—Religious aspects—Christianity. I. Title.
BV4597.53.C62S26 2012
241'.3—dc23   2012002133

Unless otherwise indicated, Scripture quotations are from the New King James Version. Copyright © 1982 by Thomas Nelson, Inc. Used by permission. All rights reserved.

Scripture quotations identified AMP are from the Amplified® Bible, copyright © 1954, 1958, 1962, 1964, 1965, 1987 by The Lockman Foundation. Used by permission.

Scripture quotations identified NASB are from the New American Standard Bible®, copyright © 1960, 1962, 1963, 1968, 1971, 1972, 1973, 1975, 1977, 1995 by The Lockman Foundation. Used by permission.

Scripture quotations identified NIV are from the Holy Bible, New International Version®. NIV®. Copyright © 1973, 1978, 1984, 2011 by Biblica, Inc.™ Used by permission of Zondervan. All rights reserved worldwide. www.zondervan.com

Scripture quotations identified KJV are from the King James Version of the Bible.

The internet addresses, email addresses, and phone numbers in this book are accurate at the time of publication. They are provided as a resource. Baker Publishing Group does not endorse them or vouch for their content or permanence.

In keeping with biblical principles of creation stewardship, Baker Publishing Group advocates the responsible use of our natural resources. As a member of the Green Press Initiative, our company uses recycled paper when possible. The text paper of this book is composed in part of post-consumer waste.

Cover design by Studio Gearbox

12   13   14   15   16   17   18   7   6   5   4   3   2   1

Contents

Foreword

The apostle Paul, speaking about the spiritual conflict believers in Christ constantly are engaged in, says these words in Ephesians 6:12: "For our struggle is not against flesh and blood, but against the rulers, against the powers, against the world forces of this darkness, against the spiritual forces of wickedness in the heavenly places" (NASB). The highly secular world in which we live finds this kind of worldview rather outdated, inaccurate and challenging to the "evolutionary progress" supposedly taking place in this hour of human history.

Make no mistake, though. We are at war. Princes and powers are real, and they love nothing better than for us to deny their influence and remain ignorant of their significance. When carnal Christians say that Paul is not speaking of the demonic realm when he teaches on it in Ephesians 6, and that these are not spiritual entities he refers to—personalities with a will of their own—I want to ask them which Christ they are following. Those who follow the Christ of Calvary, the Christ of the gospels, will engage their archenemies by wrestling with them in their walk in the Spirit. The Greek word *arche*, translated in the verse above as "rulers" or "principalities," refers to those entities that have the highest rank in hell's government under their leader, Satan.

Having said these things, I want you to realize that you hold in your hands a very powerful book written by a dear friend, Steve Sampson, entitled *Confronting Jezebel: Discerning and Defeating the Spirit of Control*. Steve did not write this book simply because he saw something in Scripture that jumped off the page. Steve has endured seasons of warfare in the Spirit over the years that God has used to season him. He is a leader who can effectively equip the saints for the work they are called to do in both the local and universal Church. One area in which the Spirit has taught Steve how to wage effective warfare involves one of these *arche* principalities—a ruler, if you will, that not only exists as a real entity in the invisible world, but that has existed throughout the long course of human history. This principality has sought to raise its ugly head against the move of God's Spirit again and again. Dare I say it is one of the most powerful entities, one of the most powerful principalities, in the kingdom of darkness itself?

Jezebel is more than the name of a wicked queen who lived at a time of great spiritual decline in the history of God's chosen people. Jezebel is also a spiritual threat to those leaders whose assignment has been to nullify this demonic principality's power in the earth. The prophet Elijah's intense battle with this principality, this archenemy, is legendary. Elijah confronted Jezebel—both the human queen and the spiritual entity—at the height of his spiritual development, destroying her organized "system" that ruled the minds and behaviors of the masses, lulling them into a drunken stupor, leaving them blinded to the truth and demands of the Only Wise God.

Jezebel's footprint appears many times in Scripture, and many times in history. Steve's treatise, now revised and updated, is a clear, clarion exposé on how this demonic principality operates and how to neutralize its power both as individuals and as a company of believers. It all begins by becoming aware of Jezebel's existence, intent and approach. From there, Steve has done a masterful job of providing keys for waging effective warfare against Jezebel. Do not expect those who have no interest in spiritual warfare to celebrate this demonic force's demise, though. They are so ignorant of their own entranced state of blindness, brought on by the power of this principality, that they cannot even recognize its effects. They need your prayers—vigilant prayers, I might add.

You, however, have picked up this powerful book for a reason. The Holy Spirit intends for you to be fully aware, fully equipped and fully furnished in this hour, because as it was in the days of Elijah, so it is today that a fresh move of God's Spirit is afoot amongst the truly hungry. God is whispering in their hearts that Jezebel must come down. So I entreat you to give heed to the words of this little book . . . it will take you a long way in the Spirit.

Dr. Mark Chironna
Mark Chironna Ministries
The Master's Touch International Church

Introduction

In the years since I first wrote *Confronting Jezebel*, I have learned a great deal more about this principality, this strongman, and how it operates. So much so that in 2010 I released a companion book, *Discerning and Defeating the Ahab Spirit* (Chosen), to help form a more complete picture of how a Jezebel spirit of control works its evil on men and women with an Ahab (passive) spirit who abdicate their God-given roles in the Body of Christ. The failure to address the weaknesses and sinful responses I talk about in both books has wreaked havoc in the lives of men and women everywhere.

In explaining the Jezebel principality, its history and how it operates, I talk about a number of situations in which controllers have operated in illegitimate authority. I also reveal the ways a Jezebel spirit of control functions through leaders in positions of spiritual authority. I place strong emphasis on how a Jezebel spirit is genderless, and I include many illustrations of this principality operating in both males and females—often differently, but without question doing its evil work in both genders.

Additionally, I underscore the truth that God purposes to dethrone every believer from the center of his or her own life. God will return for a Church without spot or wrinkle—unspotted by the work of the flesh and unwrinkled by self-will. The Holy Spirit is dealing with blatant self-centeredness and selfishness in individual lives. Ultimately, our flesh must be ruled by God and put under subjection to the Holy Spirit.

All Christians must face up to the fact that their real battle is with their flesh. The power of the flesh, which is capable of opposing the Holy Spirit in all He wants to do, far exceeds the "power" of the enemy. Jesus has already dealt a death blow to Satan! Now He desires to rule from the throne He has established at the center of our lives. All flesh must submit to His Kingship. He is Lord.

God's goal for each of us is maturity. He works with us to bring us to the fullness of His likeness,

> That we should no longer be children, tossed to and fro and carried about with every wind of doctrine, by the trickery of men, in the cunning craftiness of deceitful plotting, but, speaking the truth in love, may grow in all things unto Him who is the head—Christ.
>
> Ephesians 4:14–15

Solomon wrote that "there is nothing new under the sun" (Ecclesiastes 1:9). And so it is with Satan's wiles; they are not new. They include twisting the truth of Scripture, fear mongering, manipulation of wounded egos and many more strategies that fill Jezebel's bag of tricks. This principality uses all these to gain control through "little Jezebels," whose mental mantra is *I am always on my mind.*

It is my prayer that as you read *Confronting Jezebel*, you will come away with a greater sense of the need for humility and grace in your life as we pull back the mask and expose Jezebel's agenda. At the end of each chapter, I have included questions for you to consider. Reexamining the truths presented in each chapter will help you never again to be taken in by those who operate under a Jezebel spirit. I have also included a brief prayer after each chapter, in which you can ask God to cleanse you of any motives or tendencies toward Jezebel-like control and to remove any blindness to such behaviors manifesting in yourself or others.

Like Jehu of old, we are riding hard to engage our enemy—remembering that Jesus has already "disarmed the powers and authorities," after which He "made a public spectacle of them, triumphing over them" by the cross (Colossians 2:15). Join me as we read and study this subject together in which our God has called us "to bind their kings with chains, and their nobles with fetters of iron; to execute on them the written judgment—this honor have all His saints" (Psalm 149:8–9).

His servant,
Steve Sampson

1

Jezebel:
The Result of Flesh in Control

A s far as the children and I are concerned, from this day on we are dead to you." These are the stinging words Angie said to her mother, Barbara, as she walked into her mother's office Friday afternoon.

Barbara, a middle-aged widow, had been the wife of a pastor for many years. After her husband died suddenly of a heart attack, she continued to pastor the long-established church, along with the help of her father, Paul (the church's original founder), and her twenty-year-old son, Joshua. On this Friday, she encountered what no mother desires or expects as her daughter marched into her office and said those angry and fateful words.

Now, over 25 years later, tragically Barbara has never seen her daughter or her grandchildren again. She laments over how she and her daughter had always been the closest of friends, enjoying a delightful relationship, eating, shopping and doing all kinds of activities together. Barbara felt as if her heart was ripped out the day Angie visited her office for the last time. Little did she know that she would never again see her daughter or grandchildren. A Jezebel spirit had executed a death blow to their relationship.

Several years earlier, Angie had married Richard. Recognizing a call of God on this young man's life, Barbara's husband took him on not only as a family member, but as an associate on staff at the church. From the beginning Richard wanted control, actually to the point of wanting to be worshiped. He loved the praises of men and continually sought compliments on his intellectual capabilities.

When Barbara's husband died while only in his forties, Richard seemingly went out of his way to bestow compassion and comfort on his mother-in-law. However, looking back, Barbara realized that his kindness covered ulterior motives. His pattern was to always "minister" to vulnerable people. Usually this involved gullible women or passive men. He always sought out the weak and befriended only those personality types who would never disagree with him. In fact, the church often encouraged Richard to organize a men's retreat, but he always refused and only spent time with a few select men. He distanced himself from everyone except those whom he handpicked.

A self-proclaimed brainiac, Richard exhibited an exalted ego that seemed to compensate for his small stature. He loved to read the Greek Bible in front of everyone. But a Jezebel spirit began to become evident when he adamantly took issue with something the senior pastor, Paul (Barbara's father), had said concerning the way the church celebrated Communion. When a board meeting was called to confront Richard, he immediately diverted all attention from his grievance—which he had made into such a huge issue—by falling on his knees in front of the aging pastor, feigning submission and declaring his "loyalty." Barbara and Joshua, the other two pastors on staff since

Barbara's husband had died, had been willing to humbly confront the young man. Instead, they found themselves watching in disbelief as Richard used his manipulative ability to dodge the issue with which he was being confronted. He turned the meeting into an opportunity to schmooze the senior pastor.

This is typical of control freaks—all their behavior is calculated to make them look good. Barbara and Joshua were caught by surprise, wondering what happened to the Richard who had been so upset over the Communion issue.

A spirit of Jezebel began to manifest even more intensely when Richard sensed that his brother-in-law Joshua (the church founder's grandson) would inevitably become the pastor of the church—a position Richard coveted. He began to sow seeds to destroy the church. Over and over he would make comments like, "This ship is going down." Finally, he began to prophesy negative predictions, adding that the church had missed its day of visitation and that the Lord was bringing judgment on it. The leadership knew better. They also knew that New Testament prophecy is for edification, exhortation and comfort, not for judgment (see 1 Corinthians 14).

When Richard was called into question over his harsh, "loose cannon" prophecies, he resigned. He claimed he could no longer be part of a church that was in such error (which meant anyone who did not agree with him). However, on the very day he resigned, he seized the church checkbook and paid himself six months' severance pay and health insurance. When the church board confronted him, they agreed to pay a severance, but they insisted on paying it on a monthly basis, not in a lump sum.

Richard was furious. At that point, he manipulated his wife into permanently severing all ties in their relationship with her mother. Typical of a person with a Jezebel spirit, he let someone else do his dirty work. He had filled his wife with his own twisted philosophies; then he coerced her into declaring those fateful words in her mother's office. In classic Jezebel modus operandi, Richard was not present himself and acted innocent—although he was responsible for the entire thing.

Jezebels always have someone else do their dirty work; then they stand by looking innocent, sheepishly asking, "What have I done?" A Jezebel can seduce another person to the point where that person is a puppet through whom the Jezebel carries out his or her perverted will. In Richard's case, he let his wife deal the death blow. Many tried to counsel or coax him into forgiving and reconciling, but he has refused to repent, therefore keeping a mother alienated from her daughter and grandchildren for nearly three decades. Although he lived a life bent on destroying the reputations of those around him, this young associate pastor commanded everyone else to repent. And although others challenged him to walk in forgiveness, his concept of repentance was for all others to bow down to him. In his mind, everyone else was in need of repentance.

This exemplifies what a Jezebel (in this case a man) can do—lives destroyed, carnage everywhere, with Jezebel always seeming to get away with it.

Ironically, Richard was "trained" by a woman in the church, Deanie, long before he met and married Angie. He had no religious background, but Deanie took him under her manipulative wing. Jezebels usually befriend those whom they want to control and then shovel their diseased concepts into their lives—along with sowing seeds of how inadequate their leaders are. Over time, Deanie stroked Richard's ego and taught him what she knew about the Bible. She loved to teach the Bible and loved the title "teacher." She was a typical pastoral "wannabe." She characterized those who crave recognition and seek a position of prominence.

At one point, Pastor Paul, the senior pastor, confronted Deanie about her doctrinal positions and inaccurate scriptural interpretations, and he asked her to step down from her position and stop teaching. Needless to say, she was quite unhappy and let him know it. She immediately put her husband, Mike, to work. Mike held a position as an elder, and at the next elder's meeting, he approached the pastor with all kinds of accusations about his leadership and the church finances. Mike was an Ahab following a Jezebel's instructions, and Deanie "stirred him up," just like Jezebel did with Ahab (1 Kings 21:25).

Mike's verbal attack against Pastor Paul was vicious. Trying to wield power, Mike demanded all kinds of specifics about the pastor's finances and salary. Pastor Paul wisely told him, "I'll show you my finances if you'll match the same giving percentage in your life that I give in mine." (Pastor Paul consistently gave 30 percent of his income to the Kingdom of God.) Checkmated, Mike backed down, and soon he and Deanie left the church—but not before hurting a large number of people. Jezebels usually network with as many people as possible to firmly establish their control. The damage to the church was irreparable (they had a lot of family in attendance), and the Kingdom of God suffered.

Deanie continued to mentor Richard, who eventually married Angie. She stood by and watched Richard's tragic manipulation of his wife, and she did nothing as they cut all ties with Angie's mother forever. How sad that a family was permanently separated through the work of a controlling Jezebel spirit.

Over the years, I have met a lot of "wannabes" such as Richard and Deanie. Some end up in positions of power by putting pressure on leaders, and often these leaders do not exercise discernment, placing people in positions they are not called to or qualified for. Some of these "wannabes" do have a call on their lives, but often, because of their own insecurity and unwillingness to wait upon the Lord for promotion, they give in to jealousy and cause strife and division.

This story of Richard and the damage his Jezebel-type behaviors caused is absolutely true, by the way. It is not a made-up example. I did change the names, however, to protect those involved. Every time I hear of a situation like this, I become more aware of how evil this Jezebel principality is and how frequently it operates in our society—both through men and women. Let's take a closer look in Scripture and find out where it came from and how it operates.

The Jezebel Principality's Origin

The commonly used term *Jezebel* is actually the name of the wicked Queen Jezebel, wife of King Ahab, whose stories are found in the Old Testament. She was the daughter of Ethbaal, a Sidonian king who made a trade agreement with Israel's King Ahab. Ethbaal means "with baal," and baal was in Jezebel's name because she was the offspring of this evil seed.

Ahab's father, Omri, the sixth king of Israel, was instrumental in trying to create a friendly relationship between nations. As a result, he formed an alliance with Phoenicia (now Lebanon) through the marriage of his son Ahab to Jezebel. The marriage was meant to seal a peace treaty between two nations, but ended up being a very costly compromise. It required that Israel follow the religious and political practices of Ahab's new wife. This meant Israel would sink further into the worship of foreign gods.

The Sidonian king (Jezebel's father) was also high priest of the goddess Ashtoreth. The Sidonians worshiped two gods, Baal and Ashtoreth. Therefore, young Jezebel was raised under two pagan deities. She became a wicked and rebellious queen who usurped the rulership of Israel. Ahab's marriage to Jezebel led to Baal worship becoming widespread among God's people. Because of the control she exercised and the tactics she used to exert illegitimate and wicked control over people, Jezebel's name has become synonymous with the principality we are talking about and her spirits of control.

As an adult, Queen Jezebel introduced her new husband, Ahab, to the forbidden worship of Baal and Ashtoreth (see 1 Kings 16:30–31). Ahab's first wicked deed was to build temples to both Baal and Ashtoreth as a token of love to his new bride:

> Then he set up an altar for Baal in the temple of Baal, which he had built in Samaria. And Ahab made a wooden image. Ahab did more to provoke the LORD God of Israel to anger than all the kings of Israel who were before him.
>
> 1 Kings 16:32–33

Therefore, Ahab and Jezebel both worshiped Ashteroth and Baal and introduced this perverse religion to Israel. Throughout history, many names are given to Ashtoreth, such as queen of heaven, goddess of holiness and goddess of good fortune. The bottom line is that whether you call it Ashtoreth or Jezebel, it is the same principality behind the idol.

A Jezebel never works alone; she is most effective with an Ahab at her side to enable the evil spirit to operate fully. Queen Jezebel functioned deceptively from within the palace, controlling and dominating her husband, Ahab, and effectively leading the nation in a thirty-year reign of iniquity. Let's look at some of the telltale behaviors that characterize Jezebel—both then and now.

She Gets What She Wants

Queen Jezebel got what she wanted, and Ahab willingly gave it to her. The clear battle with the Jezebel principality is always over the domination of people. This principality desires to rule and control the people of God. If we are not people of decision and discernment, we will fall under its manipulative spell. Its agenda is one that exalts position over character.

There is something so stubborn, so mean-spirited, so jealous and so determined in a Jezebel that seemingly nothing will stop such a person from getting what he or she wants. Look at the significant instance when Ahab desired a vineyard next to his palace. A man named Naboth owned it, and Ahab was upset when Naboth refused to sell it because it had been in his family a long time. Ahab dealt with his disappointment by going to bed and refusing to eat:

> So Ahab went into his house sullen and displeased because of the word which Naboth the Jezreelite had spoken to him; for he had said, "I will not give you the inheritance of my fathers." And he lay down on his bed, and turned away his face, and would eat no food.
>
> 1 Kings 21:4

She Quickly Seizes Control

Queen Jezebel quickly took things into her own hands and seized the opportunity to exercise control over her husband, beginning her evil work:

> But Jezebel his wife came to him, and said to him, "Why is your spirit so sullen that you eat no food?"
>
> He said to her, "Because I spoke to Naboth the Jezreelite, and said to him, 'Give me your vineyard for money; or else, if it pleases you, I will give you another vineyard for it.' And he answered, 'I will not give you my vineyard.'"
>
> Then Jezebel his wife said to him, "You now exercise authority over Israel! Arise, eat food, and let your heart be cheerful; I will give you the vineyard of Naboth the Jezreelite."
>
> 1 Kings 21:5–7

Jezebel quickly appointed herself to do what her husband was not "king enough" to do. Jezebels have absolutely no regard for godly authority. Their spirit is set against the will of God. Their will has become their god and must be accomplished, regardless of the consequences. No price is too great, no life too precious if it stands in the way of their agenda. Their theology is that the end justifies the means; they will condone sin and even murder to accomplish their wishes. Basically, the Jezebel principality has no conscience. Those under its control have hardened their hearts, and their consciences are seared. Their will is king, and they are supreme.

Today in churches, families, boardrooms and marketplaces, those with a spirit of Jezebel (both males and females) have no regard for the dignity of life—no conscience. Jezebel will go to any length to get its own way, unconcerned about the lives it destroys in the process.

She Operates in Illegitimate Authority

The most dastardly expression of those with a Jezebel spirit is the way they usurp authority that is not their own. Queen Jezebel did this by writing letters in Ahab's name:

> And she wrote letters in Ahab's name, sealed them with his seal, and sent the letters to the elders and the nobles who were dwelling in the city with Naboth. She wrote in the letters, saying,
> Proclaim a fast, and seat Naboth with high honor among the people; and seat two men, scoundrels, before him to bear witness against him, saying, "You have blasphemed God and the king." Then take him out, and stone him, that he may die.
>
> 1 Kings 21:8–10

Not only did the queen steal the king's authority, but she also manipulated those in leadership. She used lies and distortions, and she even used a religious occasion and term, *fasting*, to bring her wickedness to pass. Jezebel is not afraid of "religion." This principality is a supporter of, and heavily influential in, religious organizations (as well as political organizations). But while Jezebel is religious, it wields its false power against the true prophetic flow of God. It hates the prophets and all prophetic ministries. It also hates repentance, humility and intercessory prayer because they come against its strongholds of stubbornness and pride.

She Gets Others to Do Her Dirty Work

This is an extremely predictable method of a Jezebel. As we saw with Richard, a person with a Jezebel spirit uses others to do the dirty work. Jezebels will commonly stir up innocent people until their emotions run out of control, then stand by and ask, "What did I do wrong?" Most assuredly, they will never take any blame for the result.

The elders and nobles of Naboth's city followed Queen Jezebel's insidious command:

> So the men of his city, the elders and nobles who were inhabitants of his city, did as Jezebel had sent to them, as it was written in the letters which she had sent to them. They proclaimed a fast, and seated Naboth with high honor among the people. And two men, scoundrels, came in and sat before him; and the scoundrels witnessed against him, against Naboth, in the presence of the people, saying, "Naboth has blasphemed God and the king!" Then they took him outside the city and stoned him with stones, so that he died.
>
> 1 Kings 21:11–13

She Spoils the Fruitfulness of Others

The saddest characteristic of a Jezebel is the way he or she destroys the fruitfulness of others. Ahab, acting like a spoiled child, wanted the vineyard for his selfish convenience. Refusing to show backbone enough to stand up to her spirit of control, he relinquished his authority into the hands of his wife. Naboth, however, simply felt he could not give up the inheritance of his fathers to the king for such a selfish reason. A Jezebel spirit desires that righteous people forsake their convictions so that it can do its religious work. Nabath would not comply, and he paid the ultimate price for it. An innocent man was killed, and Naboth's fruitfulness ended.

Jezebel Spirit or Control Freak?

Is Jezebel a demon—or merely a person who has controlling tendencies? Clearly, Jezebel is an evil entity that finds access to people who have not crucified their flesh. Living in the flesh sets a person up to continually come under Jezebel's control and influence. People who refuse to submit to God and insist on being in control make themselves available to this principality—the same one that animated Queen Jezebel and thus is still named for her.

Keep in mind that Satan always attempts to counterfeit the work of God. Our Father and the Lord Jesus are enthroned in heaven and operate by placing the Holy Spirit in believers' hearts, who then walk in the Spirit and carry out the will of God. The Jezebel principality operates by looking for human sinfulness and weakness in people's hearts. It then assigns and empowers evil spirits of control underneath it to do its bidding in such people's lives. These spirits, depending on the strength afforded them by the sinful, compromising lifestyles of the people they are assigned to, can oppress, seduce and partially bind them.

Paul listed witchcraft as one of the "works of the flesh" (Galatians 5:19–20, KJV). Witchcraft definitely involves manipulation. Jezebel control is behavior that operates through a person to control others by the use of manipulative, domineering and intimidating tactics. Jezebel-type controllers are almost always motivated by extreme insecurity. They are usually very wounded people (probably going back to childhood), and they operate in a protective mode of "I'm never going to be hurt or rejected again." Because of their insecurity, they seek preeminence, affirmation, power and recognition—but in very illegitimate ways.

Not all control freaks, however, are Jezebels. Control freaks tend to want to control their *own* lives, while demons operating through the weakness of someone's flesh want to exercise ungodly, manipulative control over *other* people. Control freaks are usually worriers, filled with anxiety and contempt for anyone who gets in their way. They are certainly capable of causing problems for others, but they can be teachable if approached in a gentle, nonthreatening way. Although they have some deep-seated woundedness, they manage to limp through life, struggling to find their identity in recognition and position.

True Jezebel controllers, however, are out to destroy. Their only agenda is to trample on anyone who gets in their way. When you are dealing with a Jezebel spirit, perversion of some kind is always present, whether it involves idolatry, extreme manipulation, perverted sex or a hatred of authority.

Jezebels also operate with an assumption of authority they do not have. They usurp authority and will not submit to authority of any kind. They do not like the fact that someone else is in authority, and they hate God's authority. Before Paul's departure to heaven, he warned leaders in the Church about those who would come in as wolves bent on destruction:

> For I know this, that after my departure savage wolves will come in among you, not sparing the flock. Also from among yourselves men will rise up, speaking perverse things, to draw away the disciples after themselves.
>
> Acts 20:29–30

Jezebel wants to control people, turning them to darkness.

Male and Female Jezebels

Although not restricted to either sex, Jezebel spirits are often acknowledged as more prevalent in women. Unquestionably, though, Jezebel functions just as proficiently through men. A Jezebel spirit has no gender. In reality, it simply works differently through a man than through a woman.

Where it functions through women, a Jezebel spirit seems to serve as Satan's answer to a male-dominated world, giving false protection to a woman who seemingly is never granted her rights or never has the protective love of a father or husband. Out of the lack of love, the woman rebels against the whole unloving system and becomes just like it. The controlled becomes the controller and the oppressed, the oppressor.

A Jezebel spirit often targets a woman and entices her to misuse her God-given gifts of intuitiveness, sensitivity and compassion. It twists her giftings and gets her to use her womanly position inappropriately, until she becomes very sophisticated in her ability to manipulate others without the use of physical strength. If she has been wounded or abused by a man, she might harbor a real hatred of men and a desire to get even. For example, such a woman may publicly say demeaning things about her husband—often clothing her comments in humor. Many men are afraid of that kind of wife because they fear her words and feel intimidated by her threats. A husband also has to deal with the fear of losing sexual intimacy, knowing that if he stands up to a manipulating wife, he may pay a great price.

A Jezebel spirit will try to take control differently in a man. God gifts men as leaders who supply strength and security. Husbands are told to give honor to their wives as the weaker vessels (see 1 Peter 3:7) and to "love your wives, just as Christ also loved the church and gave Himself for her" (Ephesians 5:25). But through a Jezebel spirit, the enemy will capitalize on a man's insecurity and possible woundedness and seduce him to begin controlling his wife and others through fear and intimidation. He may become very dominant in the marriage, using verbal threats and displaying occasional outbursts of temper or rage.

In his place of authority, perhaps in his workplace, groups he belongs to or even his church, a male Jezebel may rule with intimidation. Even a pastor, if he has deep insecurities, can isolate himself and become a tyrant with no input from or accountability to anyone. At the same time, he may develop soul ties with certain women in the church, developing flirtatious relationships that can ultimately lead to his downfall. (Granted, this could be the result of his own lust in some cases—but it also could be the work of a Jezebel spirit.)

The Jezebel principality achieves great effectiveness working through human nature. Once a Jezebel spirit finds a man or woman whose flesh is unsubmitted to God (especially if the person is also wounded), it moves in, and we begin to see the patterns of manipulative and controlling behavior that the well-known Queen Jezebel of old displayed. In the next chapter, we will examine more of the Jezebel principality's sinister strategies and effects.

Questions to Consider

1. Who was Queen Jezebel, and where did the Jezebel principality originate?
2. What is the difference between a Jezebel controller and a control freak?
3. Explain how a Jezebel spirit operates differently through a male and a female.

Prayer

Father, please give me eyes to see my own fears and insecurities, and the grace to keep my motives pure. Lead me into freedom from any propensity to control others or to have my own way. In Jesus' name, Amen.

2

The Sinister Strategies of Jezebel

The spiritual world, with its opposing forces of good and evil, is a world that is in one sense more real and relevant than the natural realm we live in. The kingdom of darkness is waging all-out war against the Kingdom of God, and the Bible tells us that as spirit beings, we are caught in a struggle between these two realms. We struggle with "unseen entities" that manifest themselves through people by influencing their thinking—and thereby their actions. In these last days of the Church, the thrust of the enemy is mighty as he tries to establish strongholds in people's minds and seduce our world to come under the control of Jezebel and other evil principalities and powers.

To understand strongholds, we first have to know they exist. Rooted in our thinking and philosophies, strongholds are in *us*, not in the "heavenlies." They come through our perceptions and involve far more than our physical senses. What we see, hear, touch, taste and smell is by no means the limit of our existence. Our "natural man" needs these senses to interact with the natural world. The dimension that resides outside our natural senses, however—the realm consisting of spiritual entities, both good and evil—is impossible to interpret with the carnal mind. A carnal person relates only to things perceived by the physical senses. Being born-again, however, gives a person the ability to see beyond the physical. It causes us, because we are new creatures, to relate to the spiritual realm.

A strictly carnal mind cannot relate to the spiritual, yet many Christians are now in that condition. They have become blinded because they have adopted only a natural, sensual view of things. They do not recognize that they are influenced by spiritual forces, both good and evil, and they do not know that there are spiritual implications behind what goes on in their lives. Strongholds develop in them, yet they only look at the surface level. According to the writer of Hebrews, such believers are guilty of not exercising their spiritual senses, and thus remain carnal and immature in their perspective:

> For though by this time you ought to be teachers, you need someone to teach you again the first principles of the oracles of God; and you have come to need milk and not solid food. For everyone who partakes only of milk is unskilled in the word of righteousness, for he is a babe. But solid food belongs to those who are of full age, that is, those who by reason of use have their senses exercised to discern both good and evil.
>
> Hebrews 5:12–14

When the enemy attempts to establish wrong ways of thinking—strongholds that hold people in spiritual captivity—carnal minds are the ideal place to start. That happens over and over again. For example, here in the United States, the kingdom of darkness strategically employs the fear of man to advocate political correctness. A huge concern over being seen as "politically correct" has paralyzed even committed Christians and has prevented them from speaking the truth. Through technology, the devil and his forces have access to the masses, and as in the days of Elijah, the majority submits and serves Baal because of the fear of man.

Political correctness has crippled many by appealing to the masses to compromise truth and erase all biblical standards. Liberal, heathen philosophers (here and abroad) fill universities with a humanistic, anti-God mindset. They operate under the Jezebel principality to shape the minds of the young—pure, innocent minds entering college, only to be told there is no God. The goal is to wash their minds of any moral standard and train them to be their own gods.

The United States is not the only culture prone to such influence, of course. The Jezebel principality operates around the world. This sinister spiritual force obviously operated through Adolf Hitler (along with anti-Semitism, hatred, murder and Aryanism), and multitudes went along with the man. Fearful of speaking up, they bowed under his control. First strongholds were established in people's thinking, then their actions followed suit. The influence of Jezebel past and present in the world's systems is obvious.

Isaiah accurately prophesied the twisted venom that we see injected into the world's systems in our day: "Woe to those who call evil good, and good evil; who put darkness for light and light for darkness" (Isaiah 5:20). Alongside political correctness, a spirit of tolerance has moved right into the Church. While believers are to be long-suffering, we must also possess a pure desire to let the Holy Spirit have total preeminence. We are guilty of tolerating Jezebel, and like Elijah, we need the Holy Spirit to instill in us a hatred for the devil and his ways. We must yield to the Holy Spirit if we are to thwart the enemy's sinister strategies, because the influence of this Jezebel principality has never been eradicated from the Church. Instead, it has enjoyed an unholy reign and seems more entrenched than ever.

Jezebel Entices and Weakens

Certainly, one of the most insidious strategies Jezebel uses to accomplish its agenda is pornography. I will talk more about that in the next chapter, but unquestionably Jezebel, along with the demons of lust, misogyny and the love of money, are behind the pornography industry. Ordinary men, as well as powerful leaders with mighty anointings, have become addicted. Usually they harbor a secret indulgence—one that keeps them powerless and ineffective. Laden with guilt and shame, they are helpless to walk in victory.

When leaders with great potential become tolerant of Jezebel's nature, they also become spiritual eunuchs, robbed of their masculinity and proper sexual expression. They are enticed and then weakened, unable to function as authority-filled believers. These are respectable men, but because of secret sin, they have become tolerant of and sympathetic to Jezebel's nature. Their prayers are those of anemic spiritual eunuchs instead of zealous, authority-filled believers.

More than ever, Satan is using "wickedness in the heavenly places" to deceive countless souls. Paul warned us that this battle is not with people (flesh and blood) but with the power of darkness: "For we do not wrestle against flesh and blood, but against principalities, against powers, against the rulers of the darkness of this age, against spiritual hosts of wickedness in the heavenly places" (Ephesians 6:12).

If we are dealing with a Jezebel spirit, we must ask God to place in us an intolerance of all its activities. We must search our hearts and refuse to relinquish our power and authority as Christians by harboring unclean thoughts in our private lives. We must let the Holy Spirit work in us until the enemy can find no place of access in our lives. Jesus said, "The ruler of this world is coming, and he has nothing in Me" (John 14:30). There also needs to be nothing in us that invites Satan and his hordes, including Jezebel, to have their way.

Jezebel Acts "Religious" and Prays

For many in the Old Testament, probably the most deceiving thing about Queen Jezebel was that she was religious and did religious things. As I said in chapter 1, she was the daughter of Ethbaal, whose name meant "with Baal." King Ahab married her against God's command, and she converted her husband (a descendant of David) into a Baal follower. The worship of Baal was idolatrous—essentially the worship of false gods and the work of one's own hands.

Queen Jezebel certainly lived up to her name. The name *Jezebel* is Phoenician in origin and specifically means "unhusbanded" or "without dwelling or habitation." This is true of those with her nature. A Jezebel spirit is independent; it cohabits with no one. The name can also be defined as "unmarried" or "uncommitted." Queen Jezebel was committed to her own self-will. Jezebel-type behavior clearly can be defined as the worship of self-will. People with a Jezebel spirit refuse to be team players or "cohabit" (willingly share power and position) with anyone unless they can control and dominate the relationship.

Like Queen Jezebel of old, today's Jezebels can convincingly act "religious." They are always jockeying for a position in the Church. Remember what God said about the Jezebel in Revelation 2:20? She "calls herself a prophetess." Male or female, people with this spirit love to act religiously, and their motive in doing so is to gain power and control. Usually they will volunteer for anything at church—with the hidden agenda of gaining power and recognition. If they perceive that you are strong and cannot be controlled, they will not "cohabit" with you in a ministry. They will probably remove themselves from your presence and approach others to malign your reputation. If they perceive weakness on your part, they will come after you with a vengeance. They always exalt position over character. That

33

is why humility is so greatly needed in the Church. The devil cannot do much with humility . . . but God can.

Individuals I have encountered who operate under a Jezebel spirit also do a lot of praying. But my question is, to whom are they praying? It appears as if they have created a god in their own minds who does not require them to follow Scriptures about agape love, humility and forgiveness. They frequently exempt themselves from extending forgiveness and proclaim themselves victims. They feel they do not need to forgive anyone because they are always the ones who have been hurt. They overlook the verse, "But if you do not forgive men their trespasses, neither will your Father forgive your trespasses" (Matthew 6:15). They feel justified in living recklessly within a stronghold of pride, stubbornness, resentment and rebellion and excuse themselves from the "meaty" requirements of Scripture. From their distorted perspective, however, they probably believe that they are following Scripture and that it is everyone else who is not.

Jezebel Hates the Prophetic

The Jezebel principality hates true prophets because they speak truth without compromise and give Jezebel no gray area in which to operate. In the New Covenant, this "prophetic voice" is in all believers: "Your sons and your daughters shall prophesy" (Acts 2:17). This is remarkable that the Lord is pouring out His Spirit on all flesh, but Jezebel hates the move of the Holy Spirit in the Church. That principality resists the revelation the move of the Spirit manifests—the witness of Jesus Christ and Him crucified.

All believers have the potential to prophesy, but not all stand in the office of a prophet. A prophet demands repentance and cuts away evil without compromise. Additionally, prophetic words come with creative power, which renders the enemy helpless. The Jezebel principality hates the uncompromising voice

34

of a prophet. Jezebel spirits cannot accomplish their agenda with a prophet around. That is why people in the grip of a Jezebel spirit always try to bring division and strife in churches endeavoring to flow in the Holy Spirit. They will resist God's authority, promote their own agenda and sow seeds of discord to get as many people on their side as possible, undermining leadership. They will criticize a strong prophetic voice because it simply goes against their agenda.

In the Old Testament, no one rose up to oppose Queen Jezebel except the prophet Elijah. Scripture records that they were always in conflict. Jezebel was Elijah's archenemy. Her hatred and malice toward him was limitless, and she devoted much time to trying to destroy him and his message.

Elijah—Willing to Confront Evil

Jezebel and Ahab's Baal worship involved worshiping false gods—the work of human hands. It also included child sacrifice, perverted heterosexual relationships and homosexuality. The prophet Elijah had had enough of it! Willing to confront evil, he called for the prophets who ate at Jezebel's table to come forth: "Now therefore, send and gather all Israel to me on Mount Carmel, the four hundred and fifty prophets of Baal, and the four hundred prophets of Asherah, who eat at Jezebel's table" (1 Kings 18:19). Then he challenged everyone present,

> Give us two bulls; and let them [the prophets of Baal] choose one bull for themselves, cut it in pieces, and lay it on the wood, but put no fire under it, and I will prepare the other bull, and lay it on the wood, but put no fire under it. Then you call on the name of your gods, and I will call on the name of the LORD; and the God who answers by fire, He is God.
>
> 1 Kings 18:23–24

The false prophets called on their god to consume the sacrifice, but nothing happened. They leaped about the altar and cried aloud and cut themselves until their blood gushed out (see verses 26–29), but still nothing happened.

Elijah repaired the altar of the Lord and called upon Him. When the fire of God fell, it "consumed the burnt sacrifice, and the wood and the stones and the dust, and it licked up the water that was in the trench." When the people saw the power of God, "they fell on their faces; and they said, 'The LORD, He is God! The LORD, He is God!'" (verses 38–39).

Next, Elijah commanded, "Seize the prophets of Baal! Do not let one of them escape!" (1 Kings 18:40). So the people seized them, and Elijah brought them to the Brook Kishon and executed them. Elijah's actions were more than simply a means of destroying false prophets. Elijah carried them out in such a way that they brought repentance to the people of God for ever following them. The nation had to repent and turn back to God! A true prophetic anointing does not just tickle ears but challenges people to turn and repent.

The battle between Jezebel and Elijah was over control of the people. If we are not people of decision, we are in grave danger of falling under the spell of a Jezebel spirit. People with Jezebel spirits want control and are good at getting their way. When you oppose them, you will pay a price. That is why so many seem to look the other way rather than boldly dealing with conflict.

Elijah on the Run

After Elijah killed the prophets of Baal, Ahab abdicated his authority to Jezebel. "Ahab told Jezebel all that Elijah had done, also how he had executed all the prophets with the sword" (1 Kings 19:1). Then he left the situation in her hands. Furious, she put a death threat on Elijah: "Jezebel sent a messenger to

Elijah, saying, 'So let the gods do to me, and more also, if I do not make your life as the life of one of them by tomorrow about this time'" (verse 2).

It is perplexing that Elijah, a mighty man of God who had just stood against 850 false prophets, ran for his life from one woman!

> And when he saw that, he arose and ran for his life, and went to Beersheba, which belongs to Judah, and left his servant there.
>
> But he himself went a day's journey into the wilderness, and came and sat down under a broom tree. And he prayed that he might die, and said, "It is enough! Now, LORD, take my life, for I am no better than my fathers!"
>
> 1 Kings 19:3–4

Jezebel used intimidation with great effectiveness—and with a vengeance. In Elijah's case, she used verbal threats so intimidating that Elijah responded to fear instead of to God.

Jezebels love to project a false sense of power, using fear and intimidation to cloud and confuse the minds of those they desire to oppress. How frequently such spirits try to wield their influence! Examples in church might be those who tell the pastor, "If you take this action, we will withhold our tithe," or leaders who tell those under them, "Submit to me or you won't have a spiritual covering." In a family setting, one might hear from a spouse, "If you don't see it my way, you can sleep in another bed," or "I'll leave and take the kids with me." In the business world, a manager might threaten, "You can forget about a promotion," or a disgruntled worker might threaten, "I'll sue this company until you go out of business." These are all improper channels through which controlling people use illegitimate authority to project power that is not really theirs.

All of us who have felt the rage of a Jezebel spirit directed our way through another person can identify with Elijah. We are in good company! Elijah was temporarily influenced by fear, which caused him to be bound by discouragement and despair. He was paralyzed by Jezebel's projected "power," but God delivered him.

Jezebel's threats so intimidated and blinded Elijah that from his perspective, it seemed that not one other person was left who was devoted to God. When God confronted Elijah, the prophet said, "I have been very zealous for the LORD God of hosts; for the children of Israel have forsaken Your covenant, torn down Your altars, and killed Your prophets with the sword. *I alone am left*" (1 Kings 19:10, emphasis added). A Jezebel spirit wants you to feel abandoned and surrender to hopelessness, as Elijah momentarily did. It wants you to lose your identity, authority and self-worth, and it wants you to give in to self-pity and a victim mentality. It can distort and twist your perspective so that you may think you are the only one standing up for the Lord.

The Jezebel principality may have caused over ten million Hebrews in Elijah's time to bow down to Baal, but God quickly clarified Elijah's perspective. He told the prophet, "Yet I have reserved seven thousand in Israel, all whose knees have not bowed to Baal, and every mouth that has not kissed him" (1 Kings 19:18). Elijah was not as alone as Jezebel wanted him to think, and neither are you and I!

Jezebel also desires to paralyze the prophetic flow of God. It had paralyzed Elijah, who surrendered to self-pity. Self-pity is clearly a conscious resignation in which a person surrenders to a victim mentality. When you see yourself as a victim, you literally enter into sin with Jezebel because you are not offering any resistance. For example, in my society, those who do not stand up against the pro-abortion philosophy and other liberal and worldly standards are in effect entering into sin with Jezebel. As I mentioned earlier, many compromise and go along with the pro-abortion (or pro-choice) philosophy and other liberal views, embracing a politically correct standard because they fear the reaction of their peers. Do not enter into such sin with Jezebel—resist! Embrace the truth instead. The way to stand against a Jezebel spirit is through prayer, a commitment to the truth and a willingness to confront lies.

Comparing Elijah and Jezebel

Let's take a look at the differences between Elijah's spirit and Jezebel's. One ushers in the power of God and brings repentance and change, as the prophet Elijah did. The other puts on a false religious front and tries to control through intimidation and deceit, as Queen Jezebel did.

Elijah demands repentance.	Jezebel hates repentance.
Elijah demands righteousness.	Jezebel opposes righteousness.
Elijah speaks freedom.	Jezebel desires control.
Elijah demands humility.	Jezebel appeals to pride.
Elijah speaks God's ways.	Jezebel uses deceit and systems of witchcraft.
Elijah wants God on the throne.	Jezebel wants self on the throne.

Judgment Will Come

God hates the Jezebel principality and will bring judgment upon it. Jezebel spirits destroy families, churches, businesses and relationships. Plainly, they destroy lives. Something that has always troubled me, however, is the way that those who yield to a Jezebel spirit seem to get away with it in the here and now. I have never understood that, yet I do believe that God in His mercy gives a person time to repent (see Revelation 2:21).

Yet I also know that as individuals, churches and leadership, we all have to take a stronger stand against Jezebel. God is often waiting for someone to stand up to a spirit of Jezebel—to confront it. Many succumb to an Ahab spirit, though, and simply turn their heads away from a Jezebel's tactics. They reason that, after all, he or she is religious and works hard in the Church. Many who are confronted by such a person follow the way of King Ahab—which at first seems like the easy way. (We will take a closer look at those with an Ahab spirit in chapter 8.) One of the greatest weaknesses among leaders facing Jezebel is their fear of confrontation. They want peace without paying the price of confronting the manipulative and controlling tactics of a Jezebel.

Here Comes Jehu!

Jehu was an instrument God could use. He had no fear of confrontation. His name, *Jehu*, means "Jehovah is He." As the newly anointed king of Israel, Jehu was given a clear command from the Lord through the prophet Elisha: "You shall strike down the house of Ahab your master, that I may avenge the blood of My servants the prophets, and the blood of all the servants of the LORD, at the hand of Jezebel" (2 Kings 9:7). Sent to fulfill the word of the Lord, Jehu killed King Jehoram and King Ahaziah, and then he went to confront Jezebel.

When Jehu arrived on the scene to deal with Jezebel and the others as God had commanded, the watchmen who spotted him reported that "the driving is like the driving of Jehu the son of Nimshi, for he drives furiously!" (2 Kings 9:20). Jehu was on a mission of zero tolerance. Like him, those who deal with a spirit of Jezebel must do so without compromise. To confront Jezebel and get results, we must be as furiously determined as Jehu was. We must be aggressive "drivers."

Jehu did not try to placate that foul spirit of Jezebel. The first horseman who met Jehu coming into the city asked him, "Thus says the king: 'Is it peace?'" Jehu replied, "What have you to do with peace? Turn around and follow me" (2 Kings

9:18). And he made the same reply to the second horseman who asked him. Then King Joram asked, "Is it peace, Jehu?" Notice Jehu's answer: "What peace, as long as the harlotries of your mother Jezebel and her witchcraft are so many?" (2 Kings 9:22).

Even Jezebel asked Jehu if it was peace, using her seductive tactics to try to influence him:

> Now when Jehu had come to Jezreel, Jezebel heard of it; and she put paint on her eyes and adorned her head, and looked through a window. Then, as Jehu entered at the gate, she said, "Is it peace, Zimri, murderer of your master?"
>
> 2 Kings 9:30–31

There was no room for compromise in Jehu, however. He refused to be seduced into a false peace. Like Jehu, we must not yield to the temptation of comfort and false peace while the Jezebel principality runs rampant in the world. We must refuse to be peacekeepers and instead become peacemakers. We must stand firmly on God's side and realize that we are dealing with an evil being. Although we must be compassionate toward the person in its clutches, we must deal it a death blow. To do so, we have no choice but to allow the Holy Spirit to show us where we are sympathetic and tolerant to the demonic force of Jezebel—not only in church, but in our everyday lives.

Surrounded by Eunuchs

Like Jezebel of old, people with a Jezebel spirit love to surround themselves with those who can be emasculated and easily controlled. Jezebels will feed their victims with spiritual pride to establish an ungodly soul tie and win their confidence. They will befriend and support controllable leaders—encouraging other followers to get behind a weak leader susceptible to being controlled. Jezebels do not care whom God assigns to a position; they just want someone in power who will take their advice. As I said earlier, they will not "cohabit" or "dwell" with anyone unless they can dominate the relationship. Many times they outwardly will feign servantlikeness or submissiveness, but inwardly they will harbor the motive of gaining the advantage.

I find it most interesting that Queen Jezebel had eunuchs at her side, men she had stripped of their manhood and authority. Many since their time have become eunuchs—slaves—to this demonic force. Jezebel spirits love to connect with those who have an Ahab demeanor—people pleasers without a backbone, who are willing to abdicate their authority and become passive and nonassertive. It was a welcome vindication to Jezebel's eunuchs, no doubt, to throw down their controlling queen. Heaven must have applauded their response to Jehu, who looked up at the window where Jezebel stood and asked with great authority, "Who is on my side? Who?" Two or three eunuchs looked out at him to indicate that they would take a stand against her (2 Kings 9:32). Jehu immediately commanded them, "Throw her down." They threw her down, and "some of her blood spattered on the wall and on the horses; and he trampled her underfoot" (2 Kings 9:33).

There is such significance in this. Those men whom the queen had castrated, humiliated and rendered powerless became instruments of her destruction. Sweet vindication! Victims of this treacherous principality must rise up in the power of God and be ruthless against it, just as these eunuchs were. Let God use you as an instrument in throwing a Jezebel spirit of control down. We must stop compromising with Jezebel and cling to the purpose of God.

When dealing with a person manifesting a Jezebel spirit, many believers make the mistake of being far too easy on it. We lack victory if we live in false peace where a spirit of Jezebel is concerned. Just as Jehu commanded Queen Jezebel to be thrown down, we must be aggressive, not soft. We must be ruthless, dealing it a deathblow without sympathy. God is going to let us cast this foul spirit down the way Queen Jezebel's eunuchs cast her down. We cannot negotiate with a "terrorist" Jezebel spirit. Although we can love the person in its grip, we must hate Jezebel and its behavior.

It is interesting to note how the word of the Lord came to pass concerning Jezebel's life: "And concerning Jezebel the LORD also spoke, saying, 'The dogs shall eat Jezebel by the wall of Jezreel'" (1 Kings 21:23). The name *Jezreel* means "God soweth." God sowed a disaster plan against Jezebel and her wickedness. After the eunuchs threw her down, Jehu used his horse to trample her underfoot. He later commanded the eunuchs to go and bury her because she was a king's daughter, but they could not accord her the dignity of a grave:

> They went to bury her, but they found no more of her than the skull and the feet and the palms of her hands. Therefore they came back and told him [Jehu]. And he said, "This is the word of the LORD, which He spoke by His servant Elijah the Tishbite, saying, 'On the plot of ground at Jezreel dogs shall eat the flesh of Jezebel; and the corpse of Jezebel shall be as refuse on the surface of the field, in the plot at Jezreel, so that they shall not say, "Here lies Jezebel."'"
>
> 2 Kings 9:35–37

God desires to bring eternal judgment on the Jezebel principality. Its influence in the Church must end. God is raising up those who will be militant against it, not only by becoming unyielding and assertive, but by living in full repentance, walking in total humility and loving truth more than popularity and reputation. Just as Jehu's commission was to rid the kingdom of the defiling, demoralizing influences of Ahab and Jezebel, a call is going forth today to those who are willing to stand without compromise and confront those same apostate spirits that need to be removed from the Church.

The New Testament Jezebel

In the New Testament, John the Baptist confronted King Herod and told him some things he did not want to hear; for example, "It is not lawful for you to have your brother's wife" (Mark 6:18). After that, a spirit of Jezebel began operating through his wife, Herodias, who brainstormed the idea of murder: "Therefore Herodias held it against him and wanted to kill him, but she could not" (verse 19).

A Jezebel spirit is strong and seeks what it wants, waiting for an opportunity. No wonder the Bible warns us to give no place (opportunity) to the devil (see Ephesians 4:27). When Herod gave a feast for his dignitaries, Herodias's daughter came in and danced. He was so pleased with her dance that he told her, "Ask me whatever you want, and I will give it to you. . . . Whatever you ask me, I will give you, up to half of my kingdom" (Mark 6:22–23). So the girl asked her mother what she should request, and Herodias, in true Jezebel fashion said, "The head of John the Baptist!" (verse 24).

Herodias could not receive correction and seek repentance; therefore, she had to destroy the one who spoke truth. She used her own daughter to do the dastardly deed. As I mentioned in chapter 1, a Jezebel spirit typically gets someone else to do its dirty work.

The same type of spirit that desired to destroy Elijah was clearly responsible for cutting off the head of John the Baptist. The same Holy Spirit who was on Elijah rested on John the Baptist, manifesting the same passion and focus. God said of John, "He will also go before Him in the spirit and power of

44

Elijah" (Luke 1:17). Jesus explained to His disciples regarding John, "He is Elijah who is to come" (Matthew 11:14). John also was a preacher of repentance. When he confronted the sin of King Herod and Herodias, she held it against him and wanted him killed—the same attitude Queen Jezebel displayed toward Elijah. History repeated itself.

The Jezebel principality hates a prophet, because the prophetic voice demands repentance and a surrender of self-will. A prophet calls people to the cross. Jezebel hates the cross because of the repentance and restoration it represents. Jesus proclaimed, "Elijah is coming first and will restore all things" (Matthew 17:11). Malachi also prophesied,

> Behold, I will send you Elijah the prophet
>> Before the coming of the great and dreadful day of
>> the LORD.
> And he will turn
> The hearts of the fathers to the children,
> And the hearts of the children to their fathers,
> Lest I come and strike the earth with a curse.
>
> Malachi 4:5–6

I believe that today God is raising up a Body of passionate believers who are not afraid to confront Jezebel and who will operate in the spirit of Elijah, preparing the Church for the return of the Lord. As part of that Body, our strategy must be one of zero tolerance. We must always stand against Jezebel and expose its tactics, wherever it operates—in the Church, the home, the marriage or the workplace.

Why Not Cast It Out?

Some might be wondering at this point why, instead of all this confronting and exposing and standing against the principality of Jezebel, we cannot just cast out the evil spirits that so cunningly grip people's lives? After all, as Christians we have authority over demons. Herein lies the problem: Although the demonic influence of Jezebel flows through a person, that person is also operating out of his or her own self-centered and stubborn flesh and functioning out of an urepentant human will. In other words, we cannot cast out the flesh—we can only stop Jezebel's influence, and that only briefly at best unless the person is willing to change his or her long-standing patterns of behavior.

The learned behavior of Jezebels is deeply rooted, and they enjoy the taste of power (although distorted) that a Jezebel spirit provides. Their personalities and demeanor often have been formed out of a lifetime of distorted thinking and being in control. Jezebel-type characteristics are so firmly entrenched in their personalities that "casting out the demon" does not address the whole problem.

It is very important to remember that in our warfare against such things, we do not "cast out" principalities—we wrestle against them! "For we do not wrestle against flesh and blood, but against principalities, against powers, against the rulers of the darkness of this age, against spiritual hosts of wickedness in the heavenly places" (Ephesians 6:12). Many misinterpret these verses to mean that "flesh and blood" and principalities, powers and rulers are mutually exclusive. In the context of these verses, however, they are not! In the same way that a person presents his or her body "a living sacrifice, holy, acceptable to God" (Romans 12:1), he or she also yields to a spirit of darkness. Both conditions require a decision on the part of the individual, and all spirits, both holy and unholy, influence people and use "flesh and blood" through which to manifest.

We defeat the influence of lies and deception coming from Satan and his forces by opening ourselves to the truth of God's Word. By speaking truth in love with the Word of God, we expose unholy principalities and cast down their strongholds in people's minds. The only way to get rid of the influence of Jezebel on someone is to bring truth against the deception the person has embraced for so long. The person must move toward repentance, but those with a Jezebel spirit usually run from repentance. Rarely will people under a Jezebel spirit truly repent and take personal responsibility for wrongdoing. Honestly, in my years of ministry I have rarely seen a Jezebel delivered. Sometimes the person becomes temporarily remorseful, but soon he or she goes back to using controlling tactics.

I am not saying that there is absolutely no hope for someone bound by a spirit of Jezebel. In the final chapter, I list several steps a person can take to gain and to keep his or her freedom. The person must fervently desire deliverance, however, and earnestly seek change. It takes genuine repentance to close the door on a Jezebel spirit and turn from the sins of the flesh that enable it to operate.

In the next chapter, we will broaden our perspective and look at the larger picture the Jezebel principality attempts to paint across culture, sex and the Church.

Questions to Consider

1. What sinister strategies of Jezebel have you recently seen operating in the world around you?
2. Why did Jezebel hate Elijah, and why did he run from her?
3. In what ways must we be like Jehu when confronting a Jezebel spirit?
4. Can we simply cast out Jezebel? Why not?

Prayer

Father, forgive me for tolerating Jezebel in any way. Open my eyes to all of its influence and strategies. I bind the stronghold it has on the minds of those in my life, my church and my community, and I release the Spirit of God to expose all of its works. I pull down every stronghold and fortress the Jezebel principality has built up in the area in which I live. I choose to humble myself and walk before You with purity of heart and mind and a submissive spirit. In Jesus' name, Amen.

3

Jezebel in Culture, Sex and the Church

The Jezebel principality always desires to assert its own will in the world. You can find this principality's handiwork in nearly every organized political system, behind the lust for power. Working behind the scenes through deception and manipulation, Jezebel weakens the authority of sincere leaders to govern effectively.

In America and other Western cultures today, Jezebel is the driving force behind a large number of issues and movements that set people and their values against the will of God. Those with liberal mindsets mock spiritual values and moral standards such as the sanctity of marriage and reserving sex for the confines of marriage, while at the same time condoning situational ethics and homosexuality—for starters. In non-Western cultures, Jezebel is hugely influential in the areas of extreme male dominance, the lack of freedom or rights for women and dictators who rule with ruthless control. Let's look a little closer at a few of these areas that I am familiar with closer to home, in my own culture.

The abortion controversy in the United States is just one example of how the Jezebel principality grossly affects my culture. The redefining of "personhood" has made a baby in the womb nothing more than cellular tissue—a "blob." Consequently, people are urged to believe that abortion is acceptable. The Church as a whole has stood against such atrocities. But in the same manner in which Queen Jezebel came against the prophetic leadership of Elijah, the Jezebel principality continues to come against the anointing of the Church. It makes every attempt to destroy the Church's credibility and relevance in the world. It seeks to minimize people's belief and confidence in a Holy God by attacking the very nature of God, which is *life*. Its influence on abortion is a strategic position of power for Jezebel. Jezebel is also behind the satanic lie that has been fed to our youth—"Do whatever feels good, and don't worry about the consequences."

Not only has the issue of abortion brought destruction to millions of lives, it has also divided a people who have been made righteous by the cross against themselves. Even church denominations now vehemently disagree on the issue of taking innocent life. And as the Church, we are the ultimate prize the kingdom of darkness focuses on for destruction. "The thief does not come except to steal, and to kill, and to destroy" (John 10:10).

The women's rights movement is another example of how the Jezebel principality uses an issue to terribly influence culture. The agenda of this movement in the United States has never been just about freedom for women. This is not to say that good has not come from the movement. Women now enjoy unparalleled parity with men and freedom like no other time in history, especially in Western cultures. They increasingly have the right to choose and to express themselves as free moral agents, within the protection of society. Less restricted and unhindered in personal and professional aspirations, they now can follow the blueprint God has placed within them. They enjoy better jobs and freedom to be in the workplace, and their contribution in education is more recognized. Tragically, however, just like many men, many women have not looked to the Word of God and to God Himself to find their true identity.

In understanding the history of the women's movement, though, you would by and large find that its motivation is more about dominance—not just gaining women's freedom, even from the dominance of men, but asserting women's "right" to dominate others. Women's rights is therefore not truly an equality issue in every situation; it is also about control through supremacy. Jezebel by its nature seeks to tower above anyone or anything else. Interestingly, this is the same characteristic Lucifer displayed in his rebellion against God. Isaiah 14:13–14 tells us what Lucifer said in his heart:

> I will ascend into heaven,
> I will exalt my throne above the stars of God;
> I will also sit on the mount of the congregation
> On the farthest sides of the north;
> I will ascend above the heights of the clouds,
> I will be like the Most High.

The five "I will" declarations in these verses are indicative of Lucifer's dominating, controlling motive. They further show the forceful violence that filled him when he decided on a path of self-determination apart from the life that he could have had in God. His declarations were more of an assertion that "I am fully determined by my own strength, my own power and my own cunning to dominate others and force my will on them."

While profound, there remains a subtlety in the devil's approach to domination. Lucifer is a defeated foe, yet in league with the Jezebel principality and others of his evil realm, he gains power by changing the focus of people away from a righteous God. The kingdom of darkness only has to influence the thinking of a few through lies and half-truths to gain a stronghold in the minds and imaginations of the whole.

Unholy Images—Jezebel and Sex

Today's popular movies and modern music are filled with violence, filthiness, sexual unwholesomeness and disrespect for authority and for the personhood of others. Nothing is left to the imagination; sexual images are graphically depicted in an effort to make sure we get the point. Like Satan, whom Genesis 3:1 described as "cunning" in his encounter with Eve in the Garden, the Jezebel principality is insidious and crafty in its use of these images. It directs, influences and gains control over people's minds through the use of images now enhanced through technology. Technological advances provide the multitudes with easy access to a flood of perverted images that overflow their rebellious and carnal minds, which have become the devil's strongholds.

In 1939, the popular movie *Gone with the Wind* became highly controversial because of one profane word in Clark Gable's famous line, "Frankly my dear . . ." Just a little over four decades later, that line seems like nothing. The degradation shown these days is almost mind-boggling in comparison. Almost everything coming at us is filled with filthy language, lewdness, violence and overall disrespect for God and others. (See 2 Timothy 3:1–5.)

Think about the sitcoms that undermine the family and male authority, which are largely written by homosexuals (with an Ahab spirit) who have found acceptance from those with a far-left agenda. Talk shows, which more and more exalt unrighteous thinking, are also ruled by Jezebel. So is much of the fashion industry. Then there's the pornography industry, perhaps Jezebel's most effective arena. Jezebel runs unchallenged through our avenues of entertainment. This principality is preeminent throughout Hollywood, which seems the most subservient of all to its agenda.

These words in the book of Revelation are apropos to the battle in this present day: "So the serpent spewed water out of his mouth like a flood after the woman, that he might cause her to be carried away by the flood" (Revelation 12:15). There is no question that this flood out of the serpent's mouth is the sinister deceitfulness and warring of the devil, as his destructive thrust "flows" through the electronic airwaves. This flood of words and forbidden images is now so commonplace and overwhelming that we live in acceptance of it. The prophet Jeremiah could have been describing our society when he said, "No! They were not at all ashamed; nor did they know how to blush" (Jeremiah 6:15; 8:12). We have become desensitized. We are no longer shocked and embarrassed by obscene talk or behavior.

The rebellious Jezebel principality is the spirit of witchcraft (see 1 Samuel 15:23). As understood from a biblical perspective, witchcraft is anything that usurps the authority and influence of the Holy Spirit in a person's life. The *World English Dictionary* defines witchcraft as "the art, power or act of bringing magical or preternatural power to bear through fascination, bewitching influence or charm." From this understanding, we can surmise that the imagery used by Hollywood and other sources precludes, or at best attempts to invalidate, the picture that the Holy Spirit desires to paint in the hearts and minds of people.

Contrary to this manipulation of others' minds, the apostle Paul repeatedly stated that he was commending himself and the Gospel to the consciences of men, not trying to manipulate, but to convince them. Like it or not, all of mankind is involved in the middle of a war. Both the Kingdom of God and the kingdom of darkness are engaged in a battle for our minds. In Ephesians, Paul described how wrong thinking and unholy living have the potential to separate a person from the blessings of God that flow through clean living and righteous thinking:

> But fornication and all uncleanness or covetousness, let it not even be named among you, as is fitting for saints; neither filthiness, nor foolish talking, nor coarse jesting, which are not fitting, but rather giving of thanks. For this you know, that no fornicator, unclean person, nor covetous man, who is an idolater, has any inheritance in the kingdom of Christ and God. Let no one deceive you with empty words, for because of these things the wrath of God comes upon the sons of disobedience. Therefore do not be partakers with them.
>
> Ephesians 5:3–7

When people engage in these things contrary to God, they miss out on the abundant life here and now. Contrary to the popular statement by the Hollywood culture that says, "We are simply imitating society in what we produce," in reality people are mimicking onscreen the depravity of their own hearts. Following their darkened hearts and vain imaginations, they give themselves over to all manner of evil, as Paul described in Romans 1:21: "Because, although they knew God, they did not glorify Him as God, nor were thankful, but became futile in their thoughts, and their foolish hearts were darkened." This verse tells us that these people indeed have a knowledge of God, but because they do not glorify or acknowledge Him and because they are unthankful, they are doomed to futile thoughts and darkened hearts. Read the rest of Romans chapter 1, which further shows the slippery slope into depravity that people who live this way are on.

The twisted use of the Internet has made available to the masses inconceivably destructive images and thoughts, which have entered the minds of males and females alike. Several countries have banned the spread of pornography and other destructive materials in an effort to limit the effect on their culture. But like its mentor, Satan, the Jezebel principality ultimately desires to replace righteous thinking with unholy images and thoughts, thereby turning individuals away from the life they could find in God.

Jezebel and the Church

Jezebel is not only visible in society; this principality comes to church! In Revelation 2:20, the apostle John talked about a spiritual woman, a so-called "prophetess," who was an idol worshiper: "Nevertheless I have a few things against you, because you allow that woman Jezebel, who calls herself a prophetess, to teach and seduce My servants to commit sexual immorality and eat things sacrificed to idols." In the early Church, as Gentiles became part of the Kingdom, they brought with them customs, philosophies and patterns of living that were not always in accordance with the godly precepts found in the Old Testament. One of these issues was their accustomed form of worship. They worshiped idols with animal sacrifices, which was similar to Jewish worship. But when Gentiles worshiped, their main departure was that they also included sex as part of their rituals. The sex was "between consenting adults"—male or female—with multiple partners if desired. (Sound familiar?)

In Acts 15:19–20, we find the apostles addressing this issue at the Jerusalem council. After the council reached an agreement, Peter issued this edict in the form of a hand-delivered letter pronouncing their judgment: "Therefore I judge that we should not trouble those from among the Gentiles who are turning to God, but that we write to them to abstain from things polluted by idols, from sexual immorality, from things strangled, and from blood."

The concern was that idol worship was tied to rebellion, iniquity (sin) and witchcraft. When these are present, the Word of the Lord is rejected. It is amazing how closely this correlates with what the prophet Samuel said in his rebuke of Saul in the Old Testament: "For rebellion is as the sin of witchcraft, and stubbornness is as iniquity and idolatry. Because you have rejected the word of the LORD, He also has rejected you from being king" (1 Samuel 15:23).

The Welsh Example

A colossal movement of the Spirit of God swept throughout the world between 1904 and 1906. It was recorded that nearly 20 percent (over 100,000) of the Welsh population was converted, and many were sent to other nations as missionaries. Many rough-and-tumble coal miners came to the Lord and experienced the baptism in the Holy Spirit. The usual pub gatherings were replaced with church attendance in record numbers. Police departments laid off officers because crime became nearly non-existent, and church attendance brought the demise of many sporting events typically held on Sundays. There was a call to prayer, and believers were united in an outward display of love and the power of the Holy Spirit.

The Welsh Revival had great impact not only on the Church, but also on secular society throughout the world because of its missionary focus. (It is also considered the influencing event that led to the Azuza Street Revival in Los Angeles.) At the forefront of the revival was a 26-year-old minister by the name of Evan Roberts. He was known for his operation in the gift of knowledge and in the prophetic when he preached under the anointing of the Holy Spirit. Deeply devoted to God, his devotion released an amazing shower of blessings to the Church. His preaching mightily stirred the hearts of people toward God.

All this came to an abrupt halt when a well-to-do woman by the name of Jessie Penn-Lewis entered Roberts's life. Penn-Lewis became a follower and supporter of Roberts. She had considered herself a Bible teacher but had never gained acceptance to any great extent. Challenged, rejected and ignored by church leaders in Wales, she somehow managed to latch on to Roberts and gain his confidence, to the chagrin of his friends. She began speaking into his life and isolating him from others. In a very short time, he became convinced that she held the "deep truths of God" for the purpose of bringing God's correction and direction to him.

Manipulated by Penn-Lewis, Roberts became convinced that he was usurping God's glory for himself. It anguished his soul and culminated in a state of deep condemnation. He let Penn-Lewis convince him to withdraw from ministry and to recant many of the tenets of spiritual understanding that started the Welsh Revival in the first place. Roberts moved into her home, where Penn-Lewis's domination over him became so controlling that she even wrote publications and letters using his name. He eventually broke free from her domination, but he never recovered all he had let go under her persuasion. A Jezebel spirit working through this woman caused his great ministry to lose all its effectiveness.

The story of Evan Roberts shows what a devastating, shocking effect Jezebel can have on people and ministry when allowed to manifest unchallenged and unchecked in the Church. I have had people approach me and state that they are "called to coach and bring correction to pastors and ministries." That "revelation" never quite sits well with me. If that "call" were true, then why would ministers need the Holy Spirit to lead them into all truth? (See John 16:13.) Why even read the Word of God, which 2 Timothy 3:16 says is "profitable for doctrine, for reproof, for correction, for instruction in righteousness"?

In a word, beware of those who believe it is their place to "help you" hear from God about your call or ministry. They probably have a self-serving agenda. The anointing is what helps you: "But the anointing which you have received from Him abides in you, and you do not need that anyone teach you . . . the same anointing teaches you concerning all things, and is true" (1 John 2:27).

How Does Jezebel Deceive?

Jezebel deceives with the right words and wrong spirit. A Jezebel spirit overcomes people through the weakness of their flesh, appealing to them through their fear, insecurity, wrong concepts of authority and the like. Jezebel will use any effective means, but some of its favorites are lust, sex, gossip, manipulation and false accusations.

In several instances in the book of Acts, the apostles going into new places met Jezebel deceivers. They dealt with them either through the gift of the discerning of spirits or by exercising their authority as believers. Peter had to confront Simon, the sorcerer in Samaria who wanted to buy the power he saw the apostles display when they laid hands on someone and the person received the Holy Spirit. Peter rebuked Simon for his evil motive and unrepentant heart (see Acts 8:9–24). Paul rebuked an evil spirit of divination on a slave girl at Philippi who kept disrupting the ministry by following Paul and crying out that he and his companions were servants of God. Angering her masters by freeing her from the spirit, Paul and Silas were beaten and thrown into prison (see Acts 16:16–24).

As is evident from these examples, the idolatry of Jezebel involves a love for power and authority. A skilled Jezebel can sense authority and wants to weaken it or take it away, as did those whom Peter and Paul met. Jezebel's idolatry is so strong that those with a controlling spirit will literally destroy others' lives, with no remorse, to gain what they seek. Just like Queen Jezebel in the Old Testament, Jezebel today is quick to shed blood and lead others into deeper idolatry than ever before.

In the next chapter, let's examine more thoroughly how those with a Jezebel spirit operate in everyday situations.

Questions to Consider

1. Name the five "I will" declarations of Lucifer.
2. How does Jezebel operate in our culture?
3. How does Jezebel operate in sex?
4. How does Jezebel operate in the church?

Prayer

Lord, I ask You to open my eyes and give me a discerning heart so that I can recognize the influence of Jezebel in my surrounding culture, in the area of sex and in my church. Help me to stand against Jezebel's devices and strategies and refuse to enable that principality in any way. In Jesus' name, Amen.

4

Jezebels in Action

Karen and Todd had raised their two children in a devout, loving Christian home. When their daughter, Mandy, was in college, she met a young man who was attending law school. As soon as Mandy met Tom, Karen told me that Mandy no longer wanted to maintain contact with her, and all their conversations became very brief. After graduation, Tom and Mandy married and moved to another city, where he began his law practice and they started a family.

When Karen and Todd would visit the young couple, Mandy would continually chide her mother and tell her she was not welcome in the kitchen. One day, Mandy flatly told Karen she did not like her coming to visit because they had nothing in common. The harder Karen tried to reestablish a relationship with Mandy, the greater their division became. It became more and more obvious that the real problem was Mandy's husband. For some unknown reason, Tom hated Karen and Todd, and he "trained" Mandy to dislike her parents and avoid contact with them. Hypocritically, he and Mandy treated his parents like royalty. Whenever his parents had health problems, Tom and Mandy bent over backward to help them. However, Mandy's parents did not even get an acknowledgement on their birthdays, and no phone calls or return phone calls the rest of the time.

When Karen and Todd visited at Christmas (if they happened to be invited), Mandy and Tom would talk to their children at mealtime but would act as though Karen and Todd were not even present. When Karen and Todd got ready to leave, their daughter and her husband would not even say good-bye, even though they lived over one hundred miles away from each other.

After many years of conflict, a minister tried to bring heal-ing. He wrote a letter attempting to reason with Mandy and Tom—citing their need to respect and honor their parents. Not long after, they all agreed to meet together and talk things out. When Karen and Todd arrived at this "meeting," Mandy began by reading the love passage from 1 Corinthians 13 and saying a prayer. Then she and Tom talked for over an hour. They called Karen and Todd failures because they only had four years of college, and they emphasized Tom's level of education and how highly recognized he was in the community. They further de-graded Karen and Todd because they did not have high-society friends like theirs and finally told them they did not act like Christians and had no love. They continued to berate them, raking them over the coals about things in the past.

The hypocrisy Mandy and Tom showed was difficult for her parents to tolerate, but for the sake of healing, by God's grace they humbly sat through the meeting. Though Karen and Todd felt disrespected and horrible, they also felt they had no choice but to apologize to make the kids happy. The minister who had encouraged them to meet helped them recognize that letting the kids vent could eventually lead to some restoration.

This whole situation involved Jezebel personified—the ul-timate in projection. Mandy and Tom projected their own selfishness, pride and disrespect onto her parents. The sad thing is that Karen and Todd had emphasized Christian character in the home Mandy grew up in, and no couple could have been more loving parents. They chose not to retaliate in response to Mandy and Tom's insults, however, because they desired to maintain a relationship with their children and grandchildren.

As Karen and Todd's friend, I encouraged them to stay engaged with their grandchildren, with whom they will have long-term relationships even after the grandkids become adults. Throughout the years, they have been diligently attending their grandchildren's sporting events. Mandy and Tom do not acknowledge their presence, talking incessantly to their own friends instead. When Karen and Todd try to engage in dialogue, the kids act irritated. They never introduce their parents to anyone, and if friends asked whether Karen and Todd are Mandy's parents, Mandy barely acknowledges the fact.

I personally do not believe Karen and Todd will ever have a normal relationship with Mandy and Tom, because a Jezebel spirit has total control of those two. How did this happen? Why would a young woman turn against her mother and father? In this situation, I am convinced that Tom operated under a Jezebel spirit. His own insecurities and feelings of inadequacy, probably along with wounds from his past, caused him to be bitter and hateful. Possibly because of an inflated ego and some rejection earlier in life, Tom developed a jealousy of and hatred for people and an ugly desire for control. He controlled his wife enough to foster in her a disdain for her parents.

In this true story, so many characteristics of Jezebel play out. (Again, note that to protect the individuals' privacy, I have changed the names and details in this and the other stories I relate.) Tom and Mandy showed a Jezebel-type disdain and contempt for others, disrespectfulness and dishonor toward others, a projection of their flaws onto others, boastfulness, pride, self-centeredness, a refusal to show gratitude and a determination to be socially conscious but not Kingdom conscious.

Employed by an Angry Jezebel

Allow me to relate another true story. Cindy and Janice were good friends. Eventually Cindy married Jack, and Janice married Sam. For many years, Cindy and Janice maintained a close relationship. Neither Cindy nor Jack felt close to Sam, but both enjoyed Janice's friendship. After a number of years raising their families, Jack's business was sold and he needed a new job. Sam owned a struggling business that had just turned profitable. He decided to hire Jack as his first employee. It was a great fit. Jack had run many businesses, had great computer skills and was a great organizer.

When Jack joined Sam's company, they began to prosper. It became obvious that he was a true asset. With Jack alongside, Sam could do the things he liked to do best, and Jack was also doing things he liked to do. It was not long, however, before Jack's new boss began to manifest the characteristics of Jezebel. He could not tolerate anyone else having the upper hand. He began to demand personal information from Jack that was clearly not his business. Jack told me that when Sam persistently pressed him for such information, he felt as if he were being raped.

When Sam wanted a new desk chair, Jack found a luxury office chair at no cost and gave it as a gift to the business. Without a thank-you, Sam demanded to know where Jack had found it. When an adjacent business was being sold, Sam was angry because Jack knew about it before he did. Anytime Jack was not quick to offer up details Sam insisted on knowing, Sam became very angry.

Jack said Sam had two tones that differed like night and day—with no in-between. One tone was sweet and nice. Sam might ask, "How was your day?" Then he would begin asking for personal information. When it was not provided immediately, he would get angry and demand it: "Whom did you go out to lunch with? What did you talk about?" He used the sweet tone to extract personal information and the angry tone to belittle people.

On one occasion, Jack had a warning dream from the Lord that indicated Sam should not hire a certain individual who was demanding part ownership in the company. The dream proved accurate and saved the company a huge sum of money. This man would have taken 40 percent of the company. As unreasonable as it sounds, Sam's anger escalated after that. He knew he had been spared great heartache, but he showed no gratitude—a trait so predictable in Jezebels. After a few weeks had passed, Sam started saying in a mocking tone, "Had any dreams lately, Jack?"

The favor of God was on Jack. Everything he did prospered. He would get airline upgrades, hotel upgrades and favor from clients, and Sam would mock him about the favor. Like Cain with Abel, Sam's jealousy ran rampant. This man was manifesting a Jezebel spirit so strongly that he could not tolerate God blessing someone else. One client whom Jack secured, whom he spent an enormous amount of time obtaining, caused the firm's profits to soar. The office had a celebration, but Sam said not one word of acknowledgement or thanks to Jack, although Jack was responsible for landing the account.

Jack also related to me that as a man with strong Christian principles and convictions, he always felt dirty when he caused Sam's company to prosper. When I heard that, I thought, *This man is prostituting himself, and the fruit of his labor is being "used" by a boss who wants to live and act like Jezebel.*

Jack performed a lot of tasks Sam did not like to do, which was a huge blessing to Sam, but he just could not see it. Instead, it became obvious that Sam had a major problem with jealousy. He began to hate Jack's work ethic and his relationship with the Lord. He cut Jack's hours in half and eventually fired him, saying he could not afford Jack's modest salary—although because of Jack's efforts, he was making a stratospheric income and the business grew fourfold!

The bottom line was that Sam's selfishness was off the charts. He was only interested in himself; he did not even care about his wife and kids. Although he enjoyed a huge income, he was extremely stingy with Janice, micromanaging every penny.

The termination of Jack's employment began to affect Janice and Cindy's relationship. At first, Janice confided to Cindy that she did not know how to deal with her husband's verbal abuse, selfishness, stinginess and control. Cindy had three dreams that indicated Janice would compromise. Soon after, Janice went to a Bible camp, where the Holy Spirit spoke to her in a dream and told her that her husband was wrong and that she should not be in alignment with his spirit of control. She wept and wept as she told Cindy about it. Then she told the dream to Sam. Being a typical Jezebel, he twisted the dream around and made everything Janice's fault. The next time she talked with Cindy, she minimized the dream and ultimately ended up siding with her husband, who manipulated her by promising her a lot of money. Janice became an Ahab and sold out to a lie because of Sam's manipulation.

In this sad account, again we see so many Jezebel traits. Sam manifested a classic Jezebel spirit. If he was not in control, if he did not get his way or if he did not come up with an idea first, he became enraged. It was all about control. In his mind, even God should not be in control. Sam displayed controlling behaviors, extreme jealousy, extreme selfishness, greed, a lack of gratitude, a refusal to compliment those who helped him and anger about God using other people and giving them favor.

Jezebel and the Executive

A friend of mine who is a business executive hired a nice-looking young woman as an office assistant. The first few days her performance seemed fine, but before long, he noticed some strange behavior. One of the first unusual tactics he observed was that she would hide important documents on his desk and then later in the day become the "hero" by finding the missing items. And when she was assigned to do anything, she always exaggerated her accomplishments. If, for example, she was told to call ten hard-to-reach clients, she would announce later that her task was done. However, it became apparent soon after that although she had tried to reach ten, she had been successful in reaching only one. This is a common characteristic of Jezebels. They live in a world of distortion and lies, projecting everything, even the smallest actions, to look grandiose. Also common in their world of distortions is the exaggeration of everything—especially their accomplishments.

This assistant would also underhandedly take credit for tasks other office workers had completed. This was only discovered later, because she so intimidated the other workers that they were afraid to complain. She wielded power over them by using her overpowering spirit to imply that she had a special relationship with the boss. She would also load them down with tasks just before quitting time. Again, the boss did not find this out until later since the other employees were too intimidated to speak up.

The longer she worked for my friend, the more obvious it became that this assistant would go to great lengths to make herself look big. Along with this, she always wanted instant praise and gratification for anything she did. Typical of a Jezebel, she would complain that she was not appreciated enough. She was also a chronic liar, another characteristic of those with Jezebel spirits. Jezebels are great liars! They can look you in the eye and be extremely persuasive and convincing. They know how to turn on the charm while stabbing you in the back. Their main objective is control and power, which they use to get what they want.

This young assistant was consumed with greed, yet disguised it in syrupy sweetness and dramatic enthusiasm for anyone she was trying to influence in her favor. Finally, my executive friend fired her for insubordination. She declared one day that she was leaving early. (She frequently came in late, as if she were an exception to any rules other employees had to abide by.) He insisted that she was needed until five o'clock. When she left anyway, screaming as she went out the door, he terminated her. The following Monday, she tried to return to work as if nothing had happened. She was so separated from reality that it shocked her to find out she no longer had a job.

Characteristic of many Jezebels, this young lady had no concept of reality. She had her lawyer write my friend to inform him that he was being sued for five million dollars. A week or so after her lawyer sent the vindictive letter, she called to wish her former employer a happy birthday. The tone of her voice sounded as if nothing had transpired. Days later, she made more accusations. She accused this committed Christian man of swearing at her, which was a blatant lie. Although the case was eventually dropped, she had made extreme charges—and yet frequently she would make a cheerful call to my friend as if nothing had happened.

The three most prominent characteristics of Jezebel my friend noticed in this woman were greed, manipulation and lying. I asked him what he thought lay at the root of her intense struggle for power and control. He said that she had once shared with him that she was the youngest of seven girls in her family and had never been disciplined by her parents. Children who are not disciplined often learn to manipulate.

Near the end of this assistant's employment, my friend learned firsthand how she handled another situation in her life.

She and her husband had a small water leak in their apartment. My friend heard her call her apartment manager from work, and he observed that a person with a Jezebel spirit takes ten ounces of power and makes it seem like two thousand pounds. They know how to project the *illusion* of power when they have none. He was appalled by the extreme anger in her tone and the threats she used when talking to the manager. At that point, the reality of her dangerous personality finally hit him. He rightly thought, *I'm next.*

This woman also had a major ability to generate hype. As is characteristic of the devil himself, she always strongly overplayed her hand. Her charm was one of her mightiest weapons. She was an attractive person and knew how to turn on extreme sweetness. But as always with these Jezebel spirits, that sweetness can quickly turn into gargantuan sourness if the targeted recipient does not yield. Remember Potiphar's wife? She tried to sweeten Joseph with her charms. When he refused, that same charm turned into bitterness, and she cruelly accused innocent and righteous Joseph of attempted rape (see Genesis 39).

In the story of my executive friend and his assistant, we can identify many traits of Jezebel. The woman overemphasized her importance, exaggerated, lied convincingly, projected the illusion of power, lived in a world of distortion and switched from charm to killer behavior when thwarted.

Jezebel Versus a Doctor

Another friend of mine, a doctor, had a young woman nearing the end of her medical-school training approach him to ask for a position in his practice. He was impressed by the way she came across as helpful, humble and teachable. He also noted that her attitude was extremely sympathetic. She emphasized her understanding when he expressed some apprehension about

69

her joining him, and she intimated that it would be no problem if it did not work out.

My friend began to feel alarmed, however, when this woman interrupted a conversation between him and a computer sales-man at a medical convention. The salesman mentioned hiring a couple of high school girls to do some typing. Overhearing this, she angrily butted into the conversation and said, "Why not hire a couple of guys?"

Her intrusion and hostile attitude upset my doctor friend, so he expressed some dismay about their proceeding relationship. When he approached her, she told him that her attorney husband had already secured employment in the doctor's city. Although she and the doctor had not finalized her terms of employment, she had moved in presumption and "encouraged" her husband, who had a passive nature, to go ahead and seek employment. This presumption and pushiness is typical of Jezebels.

Hearing this news, the doctor agreed to let her come on staff since her husband was already relocating. He did not feel totally right about it, but he also felt he no longer could say no—even though the woman and her manipulated husband had had no right to proceed without an official contract of employment.

After she came on staff, the doctor began to sense a constant undermining of his authority. In subtle and sometimes not so subtle ways, she began challenging his every decision. In morning meetings, she would make statements such as, "I had trouble with the way you handled that client yesterday." Undermining is typical of a Jezebel spirit, which rebels against all authority and tries to illegitimately put itself in the position of authority. The doctor tried to pass off her behavior many times, but he kept thinking, *I'm the one who hired her, and I'm the one who's been in practice for twenty years. Who is she to be challenging me?*

Soon the woman began making continual demands for the doctor to back her work more, and she constantly asked for more authority—as if she were the owner of the medical practice. The practice went through seven employees in one year, although the doctor had never had employee turnover problems in the past. This woman would correct other employees in a way that greatly upset them. My friend tried to encourage his other employees to shake it off, but one by one each resigned.

Later, employees who were intimidated and fearful of her told the doctor about how she demanded that they do procedures a certain way. They would tell her that the doctor had told them another specific way, and she would always say, "That's all right; do it my way and I'll talk to him about it." Often this upset the employees and even made some cry, but none felt they could approach the doctor because she made them think he was in total agreement with her.

This woman also began to make subtle derogatory remarks about the doctor's wife and son, but it was not until much later that the doctor realized what was going on. She was sowing seeds of discord to try to damage his family. Looking back, my friend remembers that every time he talked with her, he felt dirty and polluted.

For months she exercised and extended her authority, like a rebellious child challenging a parent to see how much she could get away with. My friend observed her with the clients. She would speak highly of clients who never questioned her, but say vile things about those who intimidated her. If people did not cater to her, or if they ever questioned her, she hated them. This is customary of a Jezebel spirit and is rooted in pride. That is why you will *never* hear a Jezebel admit any wrongdoing. It is always another person's fault.

On many occasions, my friend would be in conversation with this woman and catch himself confiding in her, giving her information that was none of her business. Also typical of a Jezebel spirit, she seemed to have a power that made him want

71

to offer information. A Jezebel spirit works that way on you, extracting information that can later be used as ammunition against you if your relationship ever ceases.

This woman also would work extra-long hours and then expect the doctor to work them as well. *He* owned the medical practice, yet was made to feel guilty for going home. She also claimed, in an article she wrote for a professional women's magazine, that she got where she was all by herself, with the help of no one else. She credited no mentor. Her love and loyalty for her boss were expressed with an evil, twisted motive for power and personal gain.

When the doctor finally caught her in an act of total insub-ordination and fired her, this woman immediately sought to destroy his reputation. She approached numerous doctors not only in that city, but in the surrounding counties. As is typical of Jezebel, she seemed to stop at nothing. Once a Jezebel loses domination—look out! Love and devotion turn into hate and destruction. It is the same spirit that wanted to destroy Elijah in Queen Jezebel's day. This person pleaded to every available listener that she was a victim, and she distorted the facts, using things against my friend that he had told her in confidence. Everything the doctor ever said to her, he told me, came back to haunt him.

Several of his colleagues would not listen to the woman be-cause her stories did not match the character of the man and physician they knew. But in this doctor's words, "She was ut-terly bent on destroying me." In her path of destruction, she attempted to steal as many of his clients and staff as possible. Two naïve students did follow her; Jezebels can be convincing.

My friend later found out (too late) that this person had a history of hating her superiors. Raised by a father whom she could never please, she felt oppressed, so she became the op-pressor. She had abandoned her former career before medical school because of a superior who had supposedly "mistreated and abused" her. In reality, she had not been abused. Rather, she was under the authority of a superior who would not put up with her manipulation and insubordination. Naturally, being a Jezebel, she would never admit that.

Can you recognize more Jezebel traits in this woman's story? She illustrates pride, presumption, pushiness, an unwillingness to admit wrong, insubordination, rebellion, sowing seeds of discord, hatred for those who dare question, intimidation and distortion of the truth.

Dating Jezebel

A graduate student friend of mine began dating an attractive young woman. Their relationship went along smoothly for the first few weeks. She loved to invite him over for meals and went out of her way to do nice things for him. Never had he been in a relationship where he had been treated so kindly and thoughtfully.

A few weeks into the relationship, however, things changed. One day he suggested that he accompany her to a nearby gas station so she could have her car tire checked. But on the day they arranged for this casual commitment, a few of his friends approached him to play basketball. When he told her that rather than making the five-minute run to the gas station with her, he would instead be involved in a basketball game, she gave him a hurt and hateful look. She would not speak to him for hours afterward. When he finally insisted that she tell him why she was so upset over a minor change of plans, she began to make vile accusations and say that he was uncaring and heartless.

This student could not believe what he was hearing as she flew into a jealous rage over his simple desire to shoot a few baskets. Her bottom line was control. Those who have a possessive,

Jezebel love want you 100 percent to themselves. Giving them 95 percent is never enough. Anyone else who requires your time becomes the enemy, and you become the enemy if you do not want to submit all your time to them.

My friend also found out months later that from the beginning, this girl had lied about herself and greatly exaggerated her past accomplishments and present abilities. She would interview him about special qualities he liked in the opposite sex; then she would *become* that person. She would make up lies about herself to make him believe she was the girl of his dreams. He was amazed at her selfishness, self-centeredness and preoccupation with herself.

She also knew how to garner sympathy. She could cry at the drop of a hat and fool almost anyone. She would milk any misfortune to the limit. Her dad had passed away after a long illness. Long afterward, she milked people for sympathy, to the point of turning failing grades from several professors into passing grades.

Further, she was an excessive braggart. To hear her family history, you would think they were of the highest royalty. She would continually compliment her features—"I have perfect facial structure and perfect teeth"—and brag about a strong grip that ran in her family. Hundreds of times, he heard her say regarding her family, "The Smiths are strong people."

She also knew how to get people out of her way. She would boldly approach people who were running for an office she desired at school and talk them out of it. She used persuasive language, saying things such as, "This is too much work for you."

When my friend sought counsel and decided to break up with the girl, she begged him not to. They were both Christians, and in his long explanation of the breakup, he stated again and again that his decision was the result of much prayer. The very second she realized his decision was made, he became her worst enemy. Her sweetness and devotion instantly turned vicious, and she declared unbelievable hatred for him. She used filthy language and called him horrible names.

For two years she worked tirelessly to destroy his reputation. Manifesting borderline clairvoyance, she seemed to know whom he was attempting to date. She would quickly befriend the young lady and distort the truth about him to such an extent that it became nearly impossible for him to get a date.

What was my friend's crime? He would not submit to this girl's every wish. She was the last child of parents who were in their mid-forties when she was conceived. She had confided that she was never disciplined and that her daddy had always given her absolutely anything she wanted. She was not accustomed to being denied anything, but my friend dared not let her have things her own way.

No one is as important to self-centered people as they are. That's why Jezebels hate the cross—the cross means denying oneself. No Jezebel wants to do that. They want power and control at any cost, no matter who is destroyed in the process.

Can you see Jezebel in this girl's behaviors? She needed to assert her own will—at everyone else's expense. Preoccupied with herself, she bragged excessively, was vindictive if thwarted and was possessive in the extreme, turning from sweet to sour in a second if her agenda went unmet.

Subject to God or to Jezebel?

While we must have compassion toward those bound with a Jezebel spirit, we must also have compassion toward those who have experienced irreparable damage through the operation of such a spirit. Therefore, we must firmly refuse to go along with any of a Jezebel's ways or controlling tactics.

God has called us to victory, and in His victory we each have freedom to make choices under His direction. We are not to be subject to the control of another person—or to a Jezebel spirit operating through him or her. Rather, we are to subject ourselves to God and be led by the Holy Spirit.

There is always hope for freedom, even for the person who has come under a Jezebel spirit and is trying to control others. God can restore any damaged life, and He can and will bring deliverance. I will talk more about that again in chapter 11, "What Can I Do about Jezebel?" Now that we have watched some Jezebels in action, though, coming up I want to provide you with a list of forty traits that those with a spirit of Jezebel consistently display. Not everyone who displays a few traits off the list is a Jezebel, but if a number of the traits line up in a certain individual's personality and keep coming to the forefront in his or her behavior, it is time to consider if something more sinister than a personality flaw is at work.

Questions to Consider

1. What are some of the things Jezebels in action do as they try to bring others under their subjection and control?
2. How does a Jezebel's devotion change if he or she is thwarted?
3. Think about whom you subject yourself to. Are you living day by day in the freedom of choice God's victory has won for you?

Prayer

Father, if there are any areas in which I have subjected myself to someone else's control rather than Your control, help me to gain my freedom in You. Help me subject myself to the Holy Spirit's leading and guiding. I also ask that You open my eyes to any behavior through which I may seek to control other people. Please forgive me for any times when I have used or disrespected others, and make my life a blessing to everyone I come in contact with daily. In Jesus' name, Amen.

5

Characteristics of a Jezebel

The character of the devil does not change, and neither does human nature; therefore, the characteristics of control remain consistent. In various situations, I have observed a number of significant traits that people with a Jezebel spirit display. The traits are amazingly consistent, although the circumstances in which they are displayed may not be even remotely related.

Before I list these traits, I want to point out that naturally, it is not fair to identify one or two of the traits in someone and determine based on those that the person is dealing with a Jezebel spirit. Each of us has character flaws and blind spots. It seems that every person has both some Jezebel traits and some Ahab traits (which I identify in chapter 8). However, when a number of traits line up in someone, it is easy to conclude that the person is dealing with the spirit and personality of a Jezebel.

Remember that Jezebel gains a foothold through the flesh, finding access and an open door in a person who has allowed his or her uncrucified flesh and selfish agenda to be in control. A Jezebel spirit is also genderless, as I have already mentioned. It can operate through a man or a woman, and it actively seeks to bring the following traits to the forefront in the person through whom it operates.

1. A Jezebel Refuses to Admit Guilt or Wrongdoing

The strongest and most evident trait of a person with a Jezebel spirit is that he or she never admits guilt or wrongdoing. To accept responsibility would violate the person's core of insecurity and pride. When a Jezebel apologizes, it is *never* in true repentance or acknowledgement of wrong. Rather, it is "I'm sorry your feelings were hurt," or "I'm sorry I spoke over your head," or "I'm sorry your face got in front of my fist." You will never hear the person say, "This is totally my fault; I take full responsibility." Always the victim, the person blames everything on someone else. He or she cannot be wrong—ever. When something goes wrong, his or her response might be, "Look what you made me do." If the person admits any guilt, it is twisted around as your fault: "I did steal the money, but it was because *you* didn't give me enough."

2. Takes Credit for Everything

A person with a Jezebel spirit is quick to take illegitimate credit for accomplishments to which he or she contributed no effort. One spouse might take credit for something the other has done, or an employer might steal the credit for an employee's contribution. Jezebels exude boastfulness and pride. In a spiritual setting, a Jezebel's comment might be, "It was my prayer that got results." The person may contribute one idea to a venture and later proclaim he or she did it all: "If it weren't for me, you wouldn't have a church."

3. Uses People to Accomplish a Personal Agenda

Selfishness and greed dominate those with a Jezebel spirit. They let others do their dirty work. A Jezebel will stir up another person's emotions by sowing seeds of division and let that person go into a rage. Then he or she will sit back, looking innocent and say, "Who, me? What did I do?" This behavior makes it difficult for even the most ardent truth seekers to pin a Jezebel down. Skillful at pushing a personal agenda, a Jezebel is difficult to deal with because he or she immediately gets defensive when challenged, attacks you and twists the facts so cleverly that you might walk away feeling confused and even guilty.

4. Withholds Information

This trait is a form of control. A Jezebel wields power over you by professing to know something you do not know. In a Jezebel's eyes, having information you lack is a powerful weapon of control. Information is power, so he or she will not offer you any but will attempt to pull information from you. Many of us can identify times when we have had relationships with such people and have found ourselves surrendering personal information to them—knowing as we gave in that the Holy Spirit was telling us to stop. This trait is so strong in Jezebels that you will experience a "pull" from them for information and a surrendering in yourself to give them confidential information. You must make a decision ahead of time not to give in. The majority of the time, the information they seek is none of their business, and they may use it later as ammunition against you.

5. Talks in Confusion

It is impossible to logically converse with a Jezebel. One pastor wrote a six-page letter to his elders about a situation in the church. The context was so vague that no one read the letter without confusion. Keeping things confusing is one way a Jezebel maintains control and domination. Jezebels may change the subject five times in one minute because it keeps them undiscovered and unexposed. They are experts at throwing you into confusion. If you confront them about a specific subject, they will skillfully divert the conversation and take you on a rabbit trail off the subject. This way, they are often able to dodge the truth and remain in charge.

6. Volunteers for Anything

Jezebels volunteer in order to establish control. They seem to have endless (nervous) energy and eagerly look for opportunities to take charge of projects. Although they will work hard, their motive is rarely pure, and eventually their secret agenda of power and control comes out.

7. Lies Convincingly

Jezebels lie convincingly. No one can lie better. They turn on the charm and make you believe blue is red. They always fool those whom they have just met, while those they have already victimized stand by helplessly. The fact that a Jezebel can look you in the eye and lie just shows how strong and adamant this rebellious, recalcitrant spirit is. One reason Jezebels are so difficult to pin down is because they have no conscience when it comes to lying. I think that because their consciences are so seared, they actually believe their own lies.

8. Ignores People

A classic ploy of Jezebels is to ignore you when you disagree with them. Leaders frequently use this tactic when someone does not agree with their plans. They isolate the person by ignoring him, choosing not even to talk to him. Some people are ignored for months just because they choose not to be a puppet and say yes to a controller's every idea or whim. Out of the leader's grace, the person is forced to either "come around" to the leader's way of thinking or be ignored indefinitely. In a controller's mind, no one is free to disagree. Jezebels are also great at using people. When they need you, they quickly warm up to you, but as soon as you have given them what they need, they will ignore you again. When they are done with you, they will throw you away like a used Kleenex.

9. Never Gives Credit or Shows Gratitude

Jezebels will rarely acknowledge another person's actions, not even for something that greatly benefitted them. They just cannot bring themselves to say thank-you or to acknowledge that someone else did something right. This puts controllers in a position of power, and they think that if they acknowledge a gift or kind action, it weakens their power somehow. They also have a sense of entitlement that makes them feel everyone owes them something. A classic Jezebel has the attitude, "You are on this earth to make me happy."

10. Criticizes Everyone

Characteristic of Jezebel, controllers always seem to disdain others and hold them in contempt. They have to be the ones who look good, so they sharply criticize anyone else who makes a good suggestion or comes up with a plan. Even if they like a plan, they will criticize it if the idea did not originate with them. Criticizing others elevates controllers in their own minds. They will also show disrespect toward a pastor, a spouse, a boss or even a close friend. They just cannot give compliments—only criticism.

11. Practices One-Upmanship

People with a Jezebel spirit will always upstage others. They brag excessively and are extremely jealous. Jezebels practice one-upmanship because they feel threatened by anyone who dares to steal their limelight. If you talk about your accomplishments, they will quickly talk about an accomplishment of theirs that is "bigger and brighter" than yours. If you say your son is on the honor roll, they will reply that their son won the Nobel Peace Prize. They will not allow anyone else to upstage them.

12. Sequesters Information

Jezebels love to control the flow of information. They want to be a walking newspaper. If a situation arises where information is important, they will push to be the first to know all about it. If you talk about an incident, Jezebels will claim that they were already "in the know" and imply that you are a failure somehow. They seem to know everything about everyone. Where they get all their information is beyond comprehension, but they can dictate data and details about people's lives in mass quantities. They relentlessly search for information, even using their children or grandchildren as "spies." You often find yourself spilling your guts to them, even though you know you should not be offering them information. Nor do they reciprocate; they only give you limited bits and pieces. They keep you in the dark because a nondisclosure policy keeps them in control. When you refuse to disclose information, they become angry and moody. Their whining response is, "Why won't you communicate?" But they do not really want to communicate; they only want to dominate and carefully control the conversation.

13. Uses Information

Jezebels use information as a leverage for power, perhaps sharing tidbits with you of things told to them in confidence.

It gives them a sense of power when they throw you a crumb of information to impress you or gain influence with you.

14. Talks Incessantly

Many people talk habitually, but those with a Jezebel spirit talk incessantly as a form of control. In a typical conversation, they do all the talking, whether it is about sports, the weather or the Kingdom of God. Because of this, they are unable to receive input from anyone else. You have no way of speaking into their lives All conversation with them is one-sided. You do the *listening*. I have seen Jezebels talk so incessantly that people absolutely cannot get a single word into the conversation. You wonder if these types are able to talk underwater! Some controlling ministers will not dialogue with you but will preach at you, as if they are afraid you will say something they cannot agree with.

15. Spiritualizes Everything

When controllers are confronted, they commonly spiritualize a situation, explaining it off on God. This prevents them from owning up to any responsibility. Since in their minds God is behind everything they do, their implication is always, "You've got a problem with this; I don't." This leaves you with no recourse—how can you speak into the life of anyone who says "God told me to" about every action they take?

16. Is Insubordinate

Jezebels never take the side of an employer, pastor or person in authority unless it will temporarily make them look good. They often will take credit for something they did not do, and they have no conscience when an opportunity for recognition presents itself. But they will not credit or recognize those in authority over them. The bottom line is that they exhibit dis-respectfulness and insubordination.

17. Is Pushy and Domineering

People with a Jezebel spirit pressure you to do things. They seem to rip from you your right to choose or make decisions for yourself. They make you feel as though you do not have enough sense to think for yourself. They will interrupt when you are getting ready to speak into a situation, and they tell you how to think, how to vote, what to eat, how to drive, the best route to take . . .

18. Operates in Clairvoyance and Mysticism

Many who operate in a spirit of control also operate in a clairvoyant spirit. The way to discern this is that they have a spirit of pride, not humility. Jezebels have supernatural help sensing information. They may use this against you and say, "I can't tell you how I know this. I just know it." It is not the Holy Spirit behind this, but the help of a clairvoyant or familiar spirit. Clairvoyance is the power to perceive things that are out of the range of human senses. It fools people by looking spiritual. When I have dealt with people who are off track, I have seen this clairvoyance operate. I would open my mouth to speak, and they would preempt me and challenge me on the very subject I was about to address. Astounded, I would be totally caught off guard because they had inside information regarding the very thing I was going to confront them about. In the natural realm, they had no way of knowing what I was going to deal with. They "knew" it supernaturally—by clairvoyance, not by the Holy Spirit. I love and appreciate the prophetic gift of the Holy Spirit, but Jezebels love to operate in this realm illegitimately, through clairvoyance and mysticism.

19. Uses the Element of Surprise

A large part of a Jezebel's main thrust to be in control involves catching you off guard. The element of surprise works well when Jezebels do things such as showing up a day early for a meeting. It is amazing how they can operate this way time after time under that demonic influence and keep you off guard.

20. Sows Seeds of Discord

Jezebels will continually belittle other people in the most subtle ways. Their strategy is to gain control by minimizing another person's value. It is common for them to tell half-truths to implicate another person in your eyes. By sowing these seeds of discord, they hope to eventually reap a harvest of destruction in others' relationships that will improve their position of power. They ignore Proverbs 6, which says that among the things the Lord hates is "one who sows discord among brethren" (verse 19).

21. Commands Attention

Jezebels like to be the center of attention; they cannot watch others be recognized and lauded without becoming jealous and hateful. They exhibit anger about God using and giving favor to someone else. When someone else is recognized, they will quickly undermine the person's accomplishments verbally. The self-centered behavior of Jezebels is self-exalting, and anyone demanding attention becomes their enemy.

22. Is Vengeful

Since Jezebels are never wrong, if you contradict or confront them, get ready to become their worst enemy. As long as you agree with them, all is well. But if you challenge them, look out! You become the target of their fiercest venom. They will stop at nothing to destroy your reputation. Amazingly, when you disagree with or thwart a Jezebel "close friend" who you thought really loved you, he or she is suddenly on a path to destroy you. Because you speak the truth, such Jezebels become vengeful, and you realize their "love" for you was really selfish, manipulative and possessive.

23. Attempts to Make Others Look Like the Jezebel

As I said, a person with a Jezebel spirit is difficult to pin down. When confronted, a Jezebel will skillfully twist the entire situation, trying to make the innocent person look like the one attempting to gain control. As always, Jezebels will do anything to look as if they are in the right. In fact, they will twist things around, distort facts and make *you* out to be the Jezebel.

24. Insinuates Disapproval

A Jezebel will often imply disapproval to those under his or her control. The controlled person feels no freedom to express an opinion for fear of disapproval, which often comes in the form of intimidation. This frequently manifests in marriage or in a working environment. Because of your experience with a Jezebel's past behavior, you fear the consequences of expressing your opinion.

25. Knows It All

Jezebels are never shy about letting you know that they are experts on most any subject. They are quick to express their opinions on anything and leave little room for anyone to point out the other side of an issue. Jezebels make idols of their opinions.

26. Is Ambitious

A Jezebel has a strong desire, but all for self. "I want what I want when I want it" describes his or her worship of self-will.

Jezebel leaders will never use the words, "We have a vision," but rather, "My vision is thus-and-so." They think the universe centers around them, and the vision has to be their idea.

27. Gift Giving

Naturally, not everyone who gives gifts is guilty of having controlling motives, but gift giving is one tactic used by those who need to control others. Jezebels use gift giving as a form of manipulation to make you feel obligated to them. They want you to "owe" them because it compromises your ability to confront them. Jezebels also can use the timing of a gift as a ploy to get you to cooperate with their agenda. Along with the gift, there can be a strong underlying current of "you owe me" or "after all I've done for you . . ." A gift is not a gift if strings are attached.

28. Is Independent

No one has input into the lives of Jezebels. They fraternize with no one—unless it is to get someone to "cooperate" with their personal agenda. They are not team players and refuse to share power and position with anyone unless they can control the relationship.

29. Acts Religious

Jezebels dwell in the local church but do not respect positions of authority unless they hold them. They are socially conscious but not Kingdom conscious.

30. Hides from True Repentance

We all want to believe a person who had a Jezebel spirit is delivered. The person may indeed seem "normal" for a time and stop exhibiting the classic traits I have listed here. Then suddenly, without warning, a situation will arise where once again that spirit is taking control and the person is wreaking havoc in others' lives. True and lasting repentance only comes when those people in the grip of Jezebel turn from living in the flesh and stop opening the door to evil. Only then will they be delivered.

31. Demands Forgiveness but Does Not Forgive

Jezebels might mumble something about how they forgive you, but because they want to maintain power, they "save" your offense to use as future ammunition. They do not totally reconcile, but hold a grudge, even though the Bible says love "keeps no record of wrongs" (1 Corinthians 13:5, NIV). Jesus was very clear when He said, "For if you forgive men their trespasses, your heavenly Father will also forgive you. But if you do not forgive men their trespasses, neither will your Father forgive your trespasses" (Matthew 6:14–15). Jezebels do not forgive because they see themselves as either a victim or as more spiritual than anyone else.

32. Cannot Receive Correction

Jezebels are so wounded and insecure that they perceive *all* correction as more rejection. They avoid rejection at all costs and will attack anyone who they perceive is rejecting them. The only thing you can give them is a compliment in a soft tone—if anything else comes out of your mouth, you are "abusive."

33. Exaggerates and Dramatizes Situations

When dealing with a Jezebel spirit, get ready for exaggeration of the facts and dramatization of the situation. When Jezebels find one person who has an issue with something they also dislike, they will turn it into, "Everyone is saying this . . ." Then they will make the case that you are the only one not in agreement with them, and that you are in the wrong.

34. Plays the Drama Queen

Jezebels are amazingly skilled at creating drama where no crisis exists. When you gently try to bring up a problem, all of a sudden they will create a huge drama, which fills the room with strife and confusion.

35. Puts Words in Other People's Mouths

Jezebels who desire position or influence will put words in other people's mouths to get what they want. They display presumption. For example, a pastor told me of a woman who asked for a certain position in the church. He politely told her he would like to seek the Lord about her request. Shortly afterward, she came and told him she was ready to start! She assumed his answer would be yes. As a young pastor, I experienced the same thing. I was naïve and trying to be compliant, and an older woman let me know that the Lord "told" her she was to be my secretary. I innocently agreed to hire her, although I did not feel right about it. The consequences were disastrous; she used the church phone to spread division among the people.

36. Masterful at Projection

Since they cannot be wrong, Jezebels will project blame on you—accusing you of behavior that sounds as if they are describing themselves. For example, if they are full of pride, they will accuse *you* of being prideful. Eliab, David's oldest brother, projected his pride and jealousy onto David: "I know your pride and the insolence of your heart, for you have come down to see the battle" (1 Samuel 17:28). And King Ahab called the prophet Elijah the "troubler of Israel," though he himself was the problem (1 Kings 18:17–18).

37. Loves Labels and Titles

Jezebels love labels and titles that make them look and sound important. They project the illusion of power. In a church setting, many Jezebels insist on being called a prophet or a prophetess. They have no humility and demand recognition.

38. Displays a Critical Spirit

Jezebels try to keep the upper hand by displaying a consistently critical spirit. If you have a new home or new car, they will make sure to tell you everything negative they can think of about it. If you like something, they will criticize it. If you dislike something, they will compliment it.

39. Loves to Vent

Controllers with Jezebel spirits have no problem "losing it" and letting you have it. Then, after they feel better, they act as though nothing has happened—while their victims are looking for a needle and thread to sew their heads back on.

40. Uses Self-Pity as a Hook

Jezebels can sulk and play the martyr better than anyone. "Why are you being so mean to me?" they might ask if you dare disagree with them. When you stand up to them and confront their behaviors, they will become extremely emotional—either with anger and accusations, or with crying and a sad disposition. They may even threaten suicide as a means of gaining sympathy and maintaining their control.

Good News about Bad Characteristics

The good news about this list of bad characteristics is that God gives each individual freedom of choice. We each have the freedom to make decisions, make mistakes, think for ourselves, communicate, decide on our likes and dislikes, express our tastes and be creative. We have the freedom to walk away from Jezebel and its influence and walk in the ways of God's Spirit.

Controllers operating under the influence of Jezebel are not free. Tightly bound by their self-centeredness, woundedness and need for power and control, they worship their own will and their own way. But we do not have to be bound by our past behaviors. Even someone with a Jezebel spirit can choose to repent and change. Thank God for the freedom to choose differently and to live in freedom, guided by the Holy Spirit instead.

Directly ahead, we will examine the extensive damage Jezebel can cause in the lives of innocent people and learn more from the Old Testament examples of Absalom, Korah and Jethro. We also will look at some specific steps pastors and others can take to prevent subjecting themselves to someone with a Jezebel spirit.

Questions to Consider

1. What characteristics of Jezebel have you most frequently seen in operation in others?
2. Have you personally struggled with any of these characteristics in yourself?
3. What is the good news about these bad characteristics?

Prayer

Lord Jesus, please reveal to me any way that I try to gain and maintain control of others illegitimately. Help me to live with pure motives and with a transparency that keeps me humble before Your Holy Spirit. Help me to admit when I am wrong and to take full responsibility for all my actions. In Jesus' name, Amen.

6

The Damage Jezebels Cause

Those who wear the label "Christian" may also be operating in a Jezebel spirit. They are often churchgoers who are very faithful in their attendance. Jesus said, "Beware of false prophets, who come to you in sheep's clothing, but inwardly they are ravenous wolves. You will know them by their fruits" (Matthew 7:15–16). Jezebels can do irreparable damage to Christians who are new in the faith. When a spirit of Jezebel begins to operate in a church, it brings division and usually results in much carnage. Sadly, many innocent people get caught in the middle, particularly Christians young in the Lord. They often do not have the maturity to discern the source of the problem (much less deal with it), and they get discouraged and leave—many times never becoming part of a church again.

When Jezebels sow discord in a church—usually out of jealousy, a lust for power and a hatred of authority—rumors begin to multiply. Often, seeds of discord sound like this: "I'm not being fed." "I want more of God than I find here." "I'm going someplace where they recognize my ministry." Not only are the spiritually young damaged when they hear such bad seed, but so are children who have listened to their parents discussing the conflict. As a result, their wounded souls will probably always place minimal value on the benefits of attending church, or they may walk away from church forever. One reason pastors' children can be so rebellious, in fact, is because they are often wounded by watching the sheep verbally attack their parents.

The danger of being the instigator behind such division is staggering. Notice the very words of Jesus:

> Therefore whoever humbles himself as this little child is the greatest in the kingdom of heaven. Whoever receives one little child like this in My name receives Me.
>
> Whoever causes one of these little ones who believe in Me to sin, it would be better for him if a millstone were hung around his neck, and he were drowned in the depth of the sea. Woe to the world because of offenses! For offenses must come, but woe to that man by whom the offense comes.
>
> Matthew 18:4–7

It is amazing that when those who sow discord decide to leave a body of believers, they always try to take as many people with them as possible. If you leave a church body, do not cause others to stumble or to leave with you. Make sure you are of the right spirit—not in agreement with a Jezebel spirit. The same Jesus who extends mercy and grace to every one of us also said to those who offend little ones that they would be better off drowned in the depths of the sea.

God hates division and clearly hates those that sow discord among the brethren (see Proverbs 6:16–19). Not only does division hurt young believers, but what about unbelievers who are watching? Seeing or hearing about division in a church may seal their decision never to turn to God.

The First "Church Split"

Those of us who have been abused by a Jezebel and consequently hurt in a church setting can take courage from the fact that the first "church split" happened in heaven. Before the creation of man, in the glories of heaven, there came a time of great rebellion:

> And war broke out in heaven; Michael and his angels fought with the dragon; and the dragon and his angels fought, but they did not prevail, nor was a place found for them in heaven any longer. So the great dragon was cast out, that serpent of old, called the Devil and Satan, who deceives the whole world; he was cast to the earth, and his angels were cast out with him.
>
> Revelation 12:7–9

Before Satan was called by that name, he was known as Lucifer. In Hebrew, *Lucifer* is *Helel Ben Shachar*. The name *Helel* literally came from the Hebrew root word *halal*, which means praise and worship. The term *Ben Shachar* means "son of the dawn" or "son of the morning," which is another phrase we see in reference to Lucifer. This Hebrew name implies that Lucifer was the chief worship leader in heaven. Yet Lucifer coveted the throne and power of God. Although he was endowed with great gifts of leadership, creativity and music, it was not enough. Why? He was full of jealousy and ambition—even in a perfect heaven. Because of this, Lucifer led one-third of the angels in a rebellion against God's authority. What a deceiver! He was able to convince angels who sat in the resplendent glory of God to believe that they would win a war against their creator.

God Loves Unity and Hates Division

God puts a high premium on unity and hates division. Starting with his rebellion, Lucifer has always striven to bring division.

After he fell, he was no longer referred to as Lucifer, but as Satan or the devil. The name *Satan* means "one who opposes" or "the adversary." No wonder when you experience a confrontation with someone who is in agreement with darkness, you can sense that opposing power—that evil that emboldens those who disregard divine order and normalcy so they can fulfill their own desires.

The name *devil* means "slanderer." One meaning of *slander* is to put oneself between two others in order to divide them. The devil attempts to put himself between God and the people He has created. Adam and Eve succumbed to the devil's lies, and the war of deception has continued ever since. Satan's goal is also to put something between people to divide them. This satanic strategy is always at work to divide church bodies, marriages and godly relationships.

Just as the enemy is always trying to put himself between us and bring division, the Lord is always trying to put Himself in the midst of us and bring unity. He wants to put His Spirit, His presence and His cross among us to unite us into one Body, His Church. Paul urged us,

> Now I plead you, brethren, by the name of our Lord Jesus Christ, that you all speak the same thing, and that there be no divisions among you, but that you be perfectly joined together in the same mind and in the same judgment.
>
> 1 Corinthians 1:10

The Door of Human Ambition

Nothing gets in the way of God's work in our lives more than human ambition. There is nothing wrong with ambition as a positive motivator, but when it is selfish ambition, nothing leads more quickly to division and strife. The nature and goal of selfish ambition is to inspire someone to seek another person's position or authority in an ungodly way. Paul warns us in Philippians 2:3, "Let nothing be done through selfish ambition or conceit, but in lowliness of mind let each esteem others better than himself." That is a hard verse to follow for those with a Jezebel spirit. Their theme is *I was always on my mind . . .*

Selfish ambition is the clearest definition of pride you can find. This is the very sin Lucifer and his angels committed trying to step out of their God-given role and usurp another role: "And the angels who did not keep their proper domain, but left their own abode, He has reserved in everlasting chains under darkness for the judgment of the great day" (Jude 1:6).

The deception surrounding selfish ambition is hardest to discern when someone actually senses a call from God but is seeking to fulfill it in the flesh. In such situations, a Jezebel spirit can get a grip on someone's heart through a lust for position and power. It is not wrong to aspire to be an overseer, to desire spiritual gifts or to show ambition in one's career. But it is wrong to covet these things to the point that you attempt to gain them through your own strength and effort, at the expense of someone else.

God's delays purge out the human ambition in us. His delays are His way of letting His Word test us before it fulfills us. We must pass the test. For example, Joseph was tested when God was preparing him for greatness. Psalm 105:17–19 relates,

> He [God] sent a man before them—Joseph—who was sold as a slave. They hurt his feet with fetters, he was laid in irons. Until the time that his word came to pass, the word of the LORD tested him.

God prepared Joseph for the palace, but he had to go to prison first. Before God's promise comes to pass, He will test what is in you and me and test our patience.

Selfish ambition in ministry causes us to start forcing doors open. Birthed through a Jezebel spirit, it causes us to operate in the arm of the flesh and not in the Holy Spirit. Ambition is usually rooted in fear, which brings striving and jealousy. "For where envy and self-seeking exist, confusion and every evil thing are there" (James 3:16).

God's delays in ministry can purge selfish ambition and save everyone heartache—if we will submit to Him. If we fight His delays instead and grasp at someone else's position, we do great damage. We need to let God bring us forth in His time. The apostle Peter told us, "Therefore humble yourselves under the mighty hand of God, that He may exalt you in due time" (1 Peter 5:6). A friend of mine used to say it this way: "If you want to go up on God's elevator, you have to push the *down* button."

Faithful, but Not Loyal

Let's look at two Old Testament examples that illustrate the treacherous selfish ambition brought on by a Jezebel spirit, the stories of Absalom and Korah. Most of us are familiar with David's son Absalom. He served forty years at the gate, hearing disputes and declaring justice. When an opportunity for power came his way, however, he proved that he was faithful, but not loyal.

Absalom was positioned as an heir to the throne. He was also David's favorite son. He had seen the injustice surrounding his sister Tamar's rape. Her violator was Ammon, another of David's sons, and David had done nothing about it. In a rage, Absalom had Ammon killed and then ran from his father, fearing David's wrath. He lived in exile for three years because David shunned him, but finally David summoned him. (David probably acted out of the compassion in his heart. He was human.)

The indifference David displayed toward Absalom by banishing him must have produced a bitterness in the young man that caused him to come up with a plan. He let the people know that if he were king, they all would have been exalted. He told the people what they wanted to hear. He challenged David's leadership, just as Lucifer challenged the place of God and Korah wanted the place of Moses (which we will look at shortly). Absalom wanted the place of his father, David.

> Now Absalom would rise early and stand beside the way to the gate. So it was, whenever anyone who had a lawsuit came to the king for a decision, that Absalom would call to him and say, "What city are you from?" And he would say, "Your servant is from such and such a tribe of Israel." Then Absalom would say to him, "Look, your case is good and right; but there is no deputy of the king to hear you." Moreover Absalom would say, "Oh, that I were made judge in the land, and everyone who has any suit or cause would come to me; then I would give him justice."
>
> 2 Samuel 15:2

Absalom feigned such a "love" for people, even kissing them. "And so it was, whenever anyone came near to bow down to him, that he would put out his hand and take him and kiss him" (verse 5). Have you ever heard someone say, "I'm going where I will feel loved"? That person had better look out, because the "loving" person over there might have ulterior motives. "In this manner Absalom acted toward all Israel who came to the king for judgment. So Absalom stole the hearts of the men of Israel" (verse 6). It is interesting that the Hebrew word for "stole" is *ganab*. It means to go in by stealth or deception.

Was Absalom ever slick. He used two tools—charm to win the people's hearts, and criticism to tear down their leader. Many were deceived by nothing more than Absalom's selfish ambition. By comparison, his father, David, had such a fear of the Lord that

101

he insisted on giving honor to the "unhonorable," King Saul. From the beginning, David sang and played his harp to soothe Saul's torment—all while having to dodge Saul's spear aimed to kill him. David could not wrap his mind around dishonoring someone who was positioned by God. He would not do it. What a difference was found in his son, Absalom. In several places, the book of Jude describes those who, out of a Jezebel spirit, act like Absalom:

> Likewise also these dreamers defile the flesh, reject authority, and speak evil of dignitaries.
>
> Jude 1:8

> These are grumblers, complainers, walking according to their own lusts; and they mouth great swelling words, flattering people to gain advantage.
>
> Jude 1:16

> Beloved, remember the words which were spoken before by the apostles of our Lord Jesus Christ: how they told you that there would be mockers in the last time, who would walk according to their own ungodly lusts. These are sensual persons, causing divisions, not having the Spirit.
>
> Jude 1:17–19

Like Absalom, those who act in such ways do not honor the position in which God has placed others. They seek to undermine their leaders. Paul referred to his ministry as "the grace given to me" (Romans 12:3). He functioned in the position to which God had called him: "According to the grace of God which was given to me, as a wise master builder I have laid the foundation, and another builds on it" (1 Corinthians 3:10). But Paul and the other apostles warned us in many places about people who would attempt to rise up and usurp the authority of God-called, grace-filled leaders:

Also from among yourselves men will rise up, speaking perverse things, to draw away the disciples after themselves.

Acts 20:30

For many deceivers have gone out into the world who do not confess Jesus Christ as coming in the flesh. This is a deceiver and an antichrist.

2 John 1:7

They went out from us, but they were not of us; for if they had been of us, they would have continued with us; but they went out that they might be made manifest, that none of them were of us.

1 John 2:19

For there must also be factions among you, that those who are approved may be recognized [manifest] among you.

1 Corinthians 11:19

Those who seek to exalt themselves in a place of ministry into which God has not yet placed them are all "wannabes" with no grace from God to render them effective. In short, they are self-willed and unyielded to the Holy Spirit.

All believers have a grace, an anointing, to operate in the segment of the Body to which they are called. It is a place for them where flowing in the Holy Spirit will produce life and fruit for the Kingdom. When we desire to be something other than what God has called us to be, however, we enter into pride and selfishness. It becomes about us and not about God, and we become self-serving.

In summary, not all who are called to love God and be part of His Kingdom respond with pure motives and a humble heart. Instead of operating in the Holy Spirit and the timing of God, out of selfish ambition some open the door to operating in a Jezebel spirit. In effect, they become instruments of the enemy.

Jesus said that it is the fruit of a person's life by which he or she is truly known. What kind of fruit is the person producing? What kind of fruit are you and I producing? It is life or death? Peace or strife? Is its focus the Kingdom of God or the "kingdom of self"?

Korah's Rebellion

Korah was another Old Testament example of selfish ambition. He manifested an evil spirit that conspired against Moses. Of course, that same Jezebel principality behind such actions is still around today, doing the same thing—conspiring against God-appointed leaders. Korah was a leader in ancient Israel and was actually Moses and Aaron's cousin. He seduced 250 other leaders to rise up in rebellion with him.

> They gathered together against Moses and Aaron, and said to them, "You take too much upon yourselves, for all the congregation is holy, every one of them, and the LORD is among them. Why then do you exalt yourselves above the assembly of the LORD?"
>
> Numbers 16:3

How many times do we hear about the undermining of God's authority in this way? Conspirators against leadership will say, "We have the Holy Spirit, too! Who put you in charge? We can hear from God ourselves!" Those who have gained a foothold in the camp and have started out in a subordinate position can cause the most harm, as Korah did, because they may have established a large following. That sounds like Lucifer and his rebellion in heaven. He had so much but wanted so much more.

Conspirators are the ones in rebellion, yet they cleverly accuse leadership of being in rebellion. Trying to exalt himself as a better leader, Korah accused Moses and Aaron of exalting themselves above the people. In fact, he tried to sound as if he were more concerned about the people than Moses was, the leader God had appointed. (It was the same tactic Absalom used.) Korah's innuendo was that Moses was a domineering personality trying to control Israel. As I talk more about in chapter 10, I am well aware that there are leaders who abuse and control. I have had my share of experiences with domineering and controlling leaders. But in many cases such as Absalom's and Korah's, it is the rebellious and abusive subordinate who wants power and control.

God knew what He was doing when He appointed Moses and declared him a man full of meekness, which is authority under control. Moses appealed to Korah in a spirit of meekness:

> Hear now, you sons of Levi: Is it a small thing to you that the God of Israel has separated you from the congregation of Israel, to bring you near to Himself, to do the work of the tabernacle of the LORD, and to stand before the congregation to serve them; and that He has brought you near to Himself, you and all your brethren, the sons of Levi, with you? Are you seeking the priesthood also?
>
> Numbers 16:8–10

Moses was appealing in gentleness, saying in so many words, "God has given you a position—why do you want mine?" He was confronting selfish ambition and that same "I want more!" attitude that rose up in Lucifer. But Korah and his followers would not honor Moses' authority, and they kindled God's anger. Moses challenged Korah and his 250 followers, and look at the result:

> The ground split apart under them, and the earth opened its mouth and swallowed them up, with their households and all the men with Korah, with all their goods. So they and all those

with them went down alive into the pit; the earth closed over them, and they perished from among the assembly.

Numbers 16:31–33

The prominent weakness in both Absalom and Korah was that neither had a teachable spirit—they both had a problem with pride. To be free from Jezebel, we must always be content to serve where God has placed us.

Jethro—A Man of Pure Motive

Moses' father-in-law, Jethro, was a wonderful example of someone with a spirit the opposite of Absalom's and Korah's. Rather than trying to usurp Moses' authority, Jethro counseled him to delegate some of it carefully to others (see Exodus 18:13–23). He spotted a way in which he thought Moses could handle his leadership role more effectively, and he approached Moses in a spirit of helpfulness, not criticism. First he stated what he saw as the problem. "The thing that you do is not good," he told Moses. "Both you and those people who are with you will surely wear yourselves out. For this thing is too much for you; you are not able to perform it by yourself" (verses 17–18). Then he suggested a solution that made good sense while honoring Moses' position and preserving his leadership:

Select from all the people able men, such as fear God, men of truth, hating covetousness; and place such over them [the people]. . . . So it will be easier for you, for they will bear the burden with you.

verses 21–22

Jethro came to Moses out of care and concern, without accusation. He was not looking to gain power for himself; he wanted things to go well for Moses and the people. Moses, who

106

had a teachable, humble spirit, was not threatened by Jethro's counsel. Many times, people with good suggestions will approach a leader in humility rather than in attack mode, simply endeavoring to see the Kingdom of God increased. Hopefully leaders will receive such input if they are humble. The result will be an increase in their effectiveness and in the unity of the Body.

The Jezebel principality works the opposite way, bringing division and strife. People with a Jezebel spirit divide a church body by airing their grievances to as many people as possible. Such people have no heart to bring unity or healing and no heart to honor a leader's position or authority. Those with such a spirit have a "religious" ambition to seek a place God has not granted them. That is dangerous territory. Scripture warns us about the behavior of men and women like these: "Woe to them! For they have gone in the way of Cain, have run greedily in the error of Balaam for profit, and perished in the rebellion of Korah" (Jude 1:11).

A Jezebel in a Church

My friend John has been pastor of a church for a number of years. As the church began to grow, one woman in particular presented a challenge to him. As we talked about his dilemma, it became obvious that she had a propensity toward control. Although she had a pure heart and a sincere desire to serve God, she also functioned out of a deep wound of rejection. Her personality disorder made her controlling—but her control was not about destroying other people, but mainly about controlling her environment. Her actions could be irritating, but she was manageable and still teachable. She was even able to laugh at herself at times. Pastor John worked with her and helped her to confront her insecurity, and she became a great blessing to the church.

Another friend of mine, Pastor Mike, had to deal with a lady in his church who was totally different. Jackie definitely had an agenda, and her controlling behavior was about accomplishing her personal agenda. In typical Jezebel modus operandi, she was always looking for ways and means to express her will and bring it to pass. When she tried to bring her own wares such as various health remedies into the church, Pastor Mike would not allow it. He had tried dealing with her on numerous occasions, but in this and other areas, she would not receive correction. She would always do exactly the opposite of whatever he said. When he confronted her, she always defended herself and would not repent; then she would approach various church members and accuse him of all manner of things, lying and sowing seeds of discord.

Pastor Mike tried to show Jackie mercy and compassion, but because of the division she caused, he became more concerned about the other church members she was influencing than about keeping her. When he would not be manipulated, she finally left the church, trying to get as many people as possible to go with her.

Months after Jackie left, the church began to grow. It did not take long for her to show up and try to weasel her way back into the church. Thankfully, Pastor Mike would have no part of it unless she demonstrated genuine repentance. Finally, he sat down with her and explained that they did not have a problem with her personally, but that as her pastor, he could not allow her to continue undermining his authority by bringing her latest "health remedies" into the church. He was trying to teach faith in God, and her behavior contradicted faith, encouraging people to put faith in her latest discovery instead of in the Word of God. As he drew these boundaries, Jackie did choose to repent, and she was able to become a blessing to the church.

One thing about people with the Jezebel spirit is that they always seem drawn to the mystical side of faith, not to the foundation of the Word. Yet it is the Word that carries God's will and His authority.

How to Deal with Jezebel

You may be asking, *What should I do once I have identified a person operating in a Jezebel spirit?* If you are a pastor, you have a responsibility to protect the sheep by dealing with these wolves that come in. In Acts 20:28–31, Paul issued a strong warning about them and exposed their motives:

> Therefore take heed to yourselves and to all the flock, among which the Holy Spirit has made you overseers, to shepherd the church of God which He purchased with His own blood. For I know this, that after my departure savage wolves will come in among you, not sparing the flock. Also from among yourselves men will rise up, speaking perverse things, to draw away the disciples after themselves. Therefore watch, and remember that for three years I did not cease to warn everyone night and day with tears.

Even if you are not a pastor, you may face the necessity of confronting a Jezebel spirit. You may be a leader in a church, a manager in business, or you may hold a position of authority in another organization. Anyone challenged by a Jezebel can take these steps to start dealing effectively with that person:

1. Do not be afraid of a Jezebel spirit, and do not procrastinate. Confront the person's behavior—it is important to strike while the iron is hot, as soon as you hear a lie or detect an attempt to usurp your authority. If you wait until later, the person will probably deny any actions or behaviors you point out.

2. Never confront a person with a Jezebel spirit alone. You need witnesses. He or she will lie and deny, and will twist and distort what you say.

3. Gather the facts. Record events and situations, along with the time and place they occur. Jezebels will try to avoid the facts and maybe even change the subject, accusing you of something irrelevant. Your record will keep the attention focused on the problem.

4. Speak the truth, speak directly and do not sympathize with the person. You are dealing with the operation of a demon. Do not be moved by crocodile tears or a dramatic show of emotion.

5. When you confront a person under the influence of Jezebel, often the demon will go into hiding and the person will act completely innocent. Do not be fooled by the deception put forth that you are "exaggerating" a behavior you know you actually observed.

6. Be aware that a person who has caused such strife and division will try to reappear later, acting very sweet but trying to once again gain influence in your fellowship. You must put into place a probationary period to determine whether his or her repentance is genuine—and it usually is not.

7. In drastic cases where the person under a Jezebel spirit has done great damage, you must issue an ultimatum. You may need to bring the matter before those who serve in authority, especially if the damage has occurred in a church setting.

Be Ready for Battle

I cannot emphasize strongly enough that when you deal with a Jezebel, you will be challenged, no matter your approach. Your best debating skills will get you nowhere. When you confront

Jezebels with the truth, they will twist it, take no responsibility and blame you. If you take a certain action, they will blame you. If you do not act a certain way, they will blame you. There is no pleasing them. You cannot please people who are under that demonic influence. Jezebels have a stubborn mindset and do not receive correction. The only thing you can do is draw a line in the sand and refuse to let such a person walk over it—or over you. You must refuse to tolerate Jezebel-like behavior.

Following a confrontation, a person with a Jezebel spirit may experience a temporary repentance and acknowledge that a problem exists. As is often the case, though, the behavior of Jezebels can be like those air-filled punching dolls that have sand in the bottom. When you knock them down, they bounce right back upright. A Jezebel spirit and the patterns of control it fosters do not let go of someone easily.

Do not be fooled into thinking all is well until you have put a trial period in place and the person who had the Jezebel spirit shows consistent change over time. Beyond deliverance from a demon, the person also must allow the Holy Spirit to bring change in his or her personality. Patterns of control often have become deeply entrenched by demonic thoughts that have formed a stronghold over time. Therefore, the person must not only resist the devil, but must continually renounce all thought patterns that formerly led to controlling behavior.

Be ready, because victory over Jezebel will require a battle. Whether you are a person who was once in its grip, or whether you are someone affected by a Jezebel, your freedom will involve a fight. Many believers are guilty of tolerance and passivity, avoiding confrontation with Jezebel at all costs, but Jezebels must be dealt with ruthlessly. Helped by the power of the Holy Spirit, we must deal with them head-on.

In the next chapter, we will talk about how a root of insecurity opens the door to the influence of Jezebel. Controllers are steeped in insecurity, which lies at the root of many of their issues.

Questions to Consider

1. What are the similarities between Absalom, Korah and Jezebel?
2. How was Jethro different?
3. Who is damaged the most by a Jezebel in the church?
4. What steps can pastors or other leaders take in dealing effectively with a person who manifests a Jezebel spirit?

Prayer

Father of heaven and earth, I am amazed that You are interested in us. You desire that we join the ranks of the humble and contrite. Help me to approach both those I lead and those I serve in that manner. When I must confront a controller, help me to be both compassionate and firm, knowing that You can bring repentance and restoration through my obedience. Strengthen me for battle through the power of Your Holy Spirit. If I have ever been the one who controlled and damaged others, please show me so that I might confess my sins, hiding nothing. Take the bitter waters out of me that would pour forth and defile others. Help me find Your great grace. In Jesus' name, Amen.

7

Controllers and Insecurity

As the popular saying goes, "If you love something, set it free. If it comes back, it was meant to be." The Jezebel principality would add, "If it does not come back, *hunt it down and kill it.*"

Two things have always plagued the Church—controllers and their desire to dominate. The power struggle these two bring on has always divided the Church and short-circuited its power. They also plague many family scenarios and can do great damage there, too, especially to children.

The desire to control and dominate, if not mastered, can lead to witchcraft. Witchcraft is nothing more than illegitimately controlling the will of another person. It is a work of the flesh (see Galatians 5:19–20) that manifests in three ways—manipulation, intimidation and domination. The desire to control is akin to witchcraft because it stands in total contradiction to the nature of God. He gave the irrevocable gift of free will to all humankind, and He Himself refuses to violate that gift. He will woo us, draw us and attempt to lead us, but He always leaves it up to us to *choose* His way: "I call heaven and earth as witnesses today against you, that I have set before you life and death, blessing and cursing; therefore *choose life*, that both you and your descendants may live" (Deuteronomy 30:19, emphasis added).

God will love people from their birth to their grave, wooing them to Himself, but He will never force His purpose on any person. He will in no way force eternal life or heaven on anyone. He honors our "right" to choose. Therefore, when people try to manipulate or dominate the will of others, it is in direct violation of God's laws and comes under Satan's domain, namely witchcraft.

Three Ways a Controller Operates

The most cunning and yet most common way someone with a spirit of control operates is through *manipulation*. This usually comes across as "If you do this for me, I'll do this for you." Manipulation *always* has a motive with it. It comes in countless forms such as flattery, self-pity, hinting for something and the like. It begins in simple ways—for example, a child who throws a tantrum to get his own way. He may manipulate his parents in front of other adults by throwing a fit at an opportune time, knowing they will not take action with company present (although they should).

In marriages manipulation takes on another form, usually manifesting through means of the silent treatment, dignified pouting or sulking. The wife may withhold sex or use seductive charms to get what she wants. The husband may withhold finances or employ countless other manipulative actions to get his way. Nothing is more repulsive than a man who puts his wife down, especially in front of others. Men who do this have such poor self-esteem that they belittle their wives to make themselves feel better.

A major power wielder with spouses is the threat of suicide. Many spouses have stayed in a destructive marriage because the selfish, manipulative and egocentric husband or wife cries, "If you leave me, I'll kill myself." Not wanting to be responsible for a death, the naïve spouse, yielding to a sickening fear, accepts this form of manipulation and decides to stay in spite of emotional and physical abuse and unprecedented misery.

In the ministry, manipulation is a tool often wielded to put guilt on people. "Send money to this ministry, or I'm going off the air and the blood will be on your hands." Or, "You must give if you expect God to bless you." Manipulation to extract money comes in many forms, but all manipulation is evil in that it illegitimately controls people. Additionally, it hinders the Holy Spirit from directing people to give money as He moves on them. The principles and blessings of giving fill the entire Bible, but people must have freedom to follow the Holy Spirit regarding where, when and how much to give.

Manipulation is the most common form of control, and Jezebels have learned to use it to get their own way. Some even train their children in it by using manipulative tactics on them such as, "If you don't clean your room, you can't have ice cream." "If you really love me, you'll clean your room." Jezebels are also overprotective and smother their children, not teaching them to interact with others properly. We have created a society of youth who have become master manipulators because they were raised in an environment of control through manipulation. Parents often give away their authority to their children. They allow the children to usurp their parental authority because they do not want to contend with the warfare they will experience by putting their foot down.

The second way a controller operates is by using *intimidation* along with fear. Intimidation usually carries with it the threat of losing something, such as, "If you want to keep your job (or remain in this marriage), you must do such and such." Anytime controlling people are unsure of their position or authority, they rely on intimidation. A boss may intimidate employees simply by raising an eyebrow, which implies that if the employees do not go along with the boss's action, there will be consequences.

Intimidation always seeks to move another person through threats. The use of fear keeps the victim under control because he or she is afraid of losing something precious. Intimidators use fear to paralyze people and provoke a specific response. Intimidation and fear are the blatant use of control through the exercise of illegitimate authority.

The third and most drastic method a controller uses is *domination*—dominating the will of another person. This is the most dastardly type of control because it leaves the controlled person no option. Husbands use this method over battered wives, not letting them out of their sight or threatening them with injury or death if they attempt to leave.

A person with a dominating personality makes his or her victims feel suffocated and literally powerless to disagree. Victims feel so controlled by the threat of disapproval, violence or scathing rebuke that they fear speaking up. Dominating controllers usually contradict everything you say. You know that no matter what your statement, they will dispute it. If you say, "It's two o'clock," the controller will say, "No, it's three minutes past two." They also continually point out tiny flaws. Their low self-esteem seems to gain a notch by finding imperfections in those around them.

Becoming a Controller

Controllers usually come from the ranks of those who have been controlled and taken advantage of. They learn it through someone doing it to them. Many times a woman who has had a dominating mother will follow the example modeled before her; a man might duplicate the behavior of his controlling father.

Many women abused by men (whether by family members or someone else) live their lives trying to get back at men because they feel they have been victimized. Living in a male-dominated world, often without real love and protection, they seek to protect themselves by becoming just like the ones they despise. Rather than feel they are being controlled, they learn to control. Their desire is to live in some fashion unabused and protected from the harshness of men, who have not been gentle and loving in their past. Their woundedness is evident, and they frequently are defensive and cold in their emotions.

Since women are not as physically strong as men, a controlling female becomes skilled at charms and seductions, temper tantrums and put-downs. Without using physical force, she can learn to position herself to stay in control. In reality, she is submitting to a Jezebel spirit, and her thoughts are structured by it. This woman may not necessarily have a Jezebel spirit at the start, but her way of thinking may help a Jezebel spirit easily find a home. Many women have, to some extent, had this thought structure put on them as they are growing up.

I should point out that if a woman has a strong, bold personality, that does not necessarily make her a Jezebel. People often mistake assertiveness for control, an error in judgment that can be very damaging to this type of woman. Scripture advocates that a woman have a quiet and gentle spirit (see 1 Peter 3:4), but this does not mean she has to be a syrupy pushover!

A controlling woman's spirit, in full maturity, is in total rebellion against God. Jezebel tries to turn everything into the opposite of what God intended. This principality so resents men that it ultimately identifies God as the source of putting men "over" women. Basically, it hates all order that God has instituted, and in its full expression, it tries to make men into women. Remember that Queen Jezebel surrounded herself with eunuchs. The Jezebel principality tries to make men into homosexuals. It seeks to turn men into women—feminizing their hair and clothes, getting them to display a lack of masculinity, an effeminate voice and so forth.

Recognizing True Ministry

A Jezebel spirit comes subtly into a church, often through a false ministry. A controlling person with a prophetic gift will use it illegitimately to gain a following of people whom he or she can control. Flattery also is used because it plays on the insecurity of others. Although there is flattery in public, there is criticism in private. People with Jezebel spirits seek to tear down others to elevate themselves. Those who love control also love recognition. Seeking recognition and authority, they want to draw people in and subsequently take advantage of them. This process is nothing more than manipulation in order to build a platform to gain control in a church.

True prophetic gifting, on the other hand, operates out of humility and accountability, not control and manipulation. True ministry never labels itself, but lets people discover it on their own. True ministers allow others to "test the spirit" to see if they are of God. If you have a genuine call of God, others will bear witness of you. Do not wear a badge. If you have a prophetic gift, let people recognize it. Do not cheapen yourself by sticking the label on yourself. Pastors sometimes ask me what title I prefer, Prophet Steve, evangelist or teacher? I say simply, "My name is Steve." "Let another man praise you, and not your own mouth" (Proverbs 27:2).

By the same token, why take it so personally if prophetic words or wisdom from God are not recognized or received? Those who take it personally will usually leave (or threaten to leave) a church because their "ministry" is not received by leadership. But have you ever seen a mail carrier sitting on the curb, crying because you are upset that you received a bill in the mail? No, he is only the deliverer of the message. The Lord revealed to me that if you are upset over how people received your "message," it is an indication that the message came from you and not from God. If it is God's message,

He should be the one who is upset, not you. You are not in charge; God is. You and I are free to obey the Lord and leave the results to Him.

How Control Takes Root

Deep insecurity lies at the root of a controlling personality. Insecurity is the deepest root cause of fear, jealousy, anger, resentment, bitterness and a need to be right.

Those plagued with insecurity carry a great sense of rejection and seek attention and approval. The complexity of insecurity and inferiority comes to a head in the desire to control. Finding feelings of inferiority intolerable, the mentality flip-flops into a sense of superiority and pride. This often occurs in someone who feels his or her physical body does not measure up. Twisted pride runs even deeper than the typical ego of an athletic jock. This person who once felt so deeply inferior now, in a perverted sense, feels superior to everyone. He or she becomes a know-it-all and is threatened by anyone who dares to disagree, seeing them as the enemy. Extremely opinionated, this person is now quick to express his or her opinion as the final authority. No other input needed, thank you!

The power of control gives insecure people a feeling of self-worth and importance. It validates their existence. Controlling behavior often begins at a young age, especially if a child is not disciplined. Most often, it develops into a lifestyle. That is why it is so rare to see those with a controlling spirit totally delivered. Controlling has become such a part of their nature that it literally becomes part of their personality. And as I said before, some may ask why this kind of damaging spirit, operating in the demonic, cannot be cast out. But simply put, one cannot cast out a personality. That is why repentance is mandatory before the demonic influence can be dealt with.

There is a consistent correlation between low self-esteem and a determination to control others. With the feeling of poor self-worth comes such a spirit of rejection that the only way the person perceives that he or she can obtain acceptance, recognition or power is through the vehicle of control. You can almost hear the controller reason, *I'm sick of low self-worth and rejection, so I will take control of every person in my path, and no one will ever make me feel this way again.*

What Motivates Controllers?

Let's look at a few of the motivations behind a controlling personality:

- They cannot bear to be wrong.
- They have a need to be elevated, so they will award themselves credit and even titles.
- They have a need to feel power and authority, and they will do anything to achieve those.
- They feel they know more than anyone else; therefore, they dominate all conversations.
- They feel no one can handle things as well as they can (not even God). Therefore, they take things into their own hands.

The following characteristics often come to the forefront in a controller's personality:

Pride

The stronghold of pride is closely tied with insecurity. Since a controller cannot stand the rejection of being wrong, he or she will more and more build up a stronghold of pride. Statements like, "I'm sorry," or "It was totally my fault," will never pass a controller's lips.

Many times I have counseled a husband or wife married to a controller. The situation is always the same. For years, the controller has never admitted being wrong about anything. The other spouse may try so hard to have peace that he or she will make up something to apologize for, but the controller will not reciprocate by saying "I'm sorry, too." In fact, often the controller's response is, "You should be sorry."

Usually the spouse without the spirit of control will talk about how many times he or she has admitted to being wrong just to bring peace. But he or she also resents how the controller, under no circumstances, will admit wrongdoing of any kind. The controller may reluctantly say words to the effect of, "I'm sorry you misunderstood me," but that admits nothing and further reinforces pride and an unteachable spirit.

Boastfulness

Boasting is closely related to pride. Controllers take credit for everything and blame for nothing. Because of insecurity and rejection, controllers feel driven to remind everyone how successful their life is, what great accomplishments their children have attained, and so on. Of course, boasters are not even remotely interested in the achievements of those listening. They are too busy desperately trying to elevate themselves in their own minds.

Fear of Rejection

Controllers are bound with a fear of rejection. Characteristically, their lives have to be perfect. Therefore, you may observe in them a strong preoccupation with looks, clothes, makeup, jewelry, cars and cleanliness. Controllers cannot bear the thought of being seen in public as less than perfect. They carefully choose their environment so that they will never be perceived by anyone as less than perfect. This, of course, is far from living in freedom.

The Need for Predictability

Controllers also desire to be able to predict things at every stage of life. Seeking predictability leads to control, because controllers manipulate their circumstances so much that they end up attempting to reposition everything in their lives—including both things and people. The less predictable a situation is, the more insecure controllers feel.

Controllers expend great effort manipulating people and circumstances so that nothing is left to chance. A simple change of plans can magnify their insecurity and put them out of sorts. They not only lack trust in God, they are often hostile toward Him. They see Him as the guilty party for not cooperating with their desire for events to unfold predictably.

Isn't Everyone Insecure?

Not everyone who is insecure is a controlling person. The truth is that we all have a measure of insecurity within us. No doubt it goes all the way back to when Adam and Eve, upon sinning, experienced insecurity and tried to hide from God (see Genesis 3). We live in an insecure world. Many of us strive to dress a certain way, to own certain possessions, to attain power and find acceptance—all to fulfill an insecure void within.

Criticism is rooted in insecurity. Criticizing others elevates an insecure person in his or her mind. Hearing other people's accomplishments praised usually causes a reaction, making those with insecurities feel fragile and like less of a person. They will quickly say something to upgrade their own accomplishments in view of what has been spoken in praise of someone else.

Insecurity needs to be taken to the cross. The security of every believer is in the person of Jesus Christ. We need to be secure in Christ and let Him deliver us from our insecurities. When we relinquish all rights to our lives and lay them at the foot of the cross, we walk away free!

In Christ we declare our helplessness and receive His acceptance, "to the praise of the glory of His grace, by which He made us *accepted* in the Beloved" (Ephesians 1:6, emphasis added). His unconditional love annihilates all rejection, and we are free in Him. No longer do we perceive His love for us as tied to our performance. His love saturates our being, and we know we are loved and accepted in spite of any flaws or failures.

If we are fearful and need to control the people and circumstances around us, we have not yet received God's love. "There is no fear in love; but perfect love casts out fear, because fear involves torment. But he who fears *has not been made perfect in love*" (1 John 4:18, emphasis added).

The Family Setting

In a family setting, the controlling parent often dominates the children and places them in the position of siding against the opposing parent. This parent controls the children's line of communication so that the other parent only gets "old news." The passive parent is basically out of the loop unless he or she is urgently needed to solve problems that the controlling parent caused.

If their parents are not on the same page, children learn to manipulate by going through one parent but not dealing directly with the other. They unknowingly violate the Scripture, "'Honor your father and mother,' which is the first commandment with promise: 'that it may be well with you and you may live long on the earth'" (Ephesians 6:2–3).

Children ultimately resent a passive (Ahab-like) parent for not protecting them in this kind of family scenario. To correct or prevent such issues, the uncontrolling parent must become assertive, asking questions and making individual time with each child, regardless of age, to stay in the loop with his or her life. The passive parent must also become willing to confront the controlling parent without fear of his or her reaction. There will be a reaction, but the children's well-being is worth the price of confronting any issues that are keeping the family from relating on healthier terms.

The Youngest Child

Sometimes the youngest child of a family develops a spirit of control simply because he or she is spoiled. Parents tend to overprotect and overindulge their youngest child, even to the point of rarely exerting discipline. Common parenting problems include letting the child get his or her way, cooking separate meals if the food the rest of the family is eating does not meet the youngest child's approval, not enforcing bedtime, withholding discipline, lavishing on the child anything he or she asks for—basically allowing manipulation to develop in the child.

Tragically, the youngest child can grow up into a classic manipulator who is incredibly self-centered. Although the child has low self-esteem (undisciplined children often have low self-esteem since they lack the loving discipline that builds self-worth), as an adult he or she will project a false sense of importance and an "I can do no wrong" attitude.

Severely spoiled children will let nothing stand in the way of accomplishing their desires. Often, while their grown siblings watch, the youngest sibling, spoiled as a child, will take advantage of aging parents. We recently counseled in a situation where the youngest girl insisted that her parents babysit her children for long periods of time, although the parents were elderly and in very poor health. When her older siblings objected, they were tongue-lashed. In another situation, the youngest sibling manipulated the elderly parents by continually asking for money for various ventures, although the parents were on a very limited income.

These youngest children generally hone their manipulation tactics over time so that they become very skilled at getting people to do what they want. Totally self-serving, they do not care whom they hurt in the process. While growing up, they learned to get their way through pouting, tantrum-throwing, sulking, threatening and intimidating. No wonder they grow up into professional controllers who use more refined tactics. By the time they reach adulthood, their controlling behaviors and an evil spirit of control are deeply rooted and firmly planted.

Why Deliverance Does Not Come

When insecure people are confronted with truth, they perceive their confronter as the enemy and counterattack. In fact, there seems to be no greater wrath than that of a controlling person who is confronted. This person will forcefully retaliate, never admitting guilt or relinquishing his or her sense of power.

Defensiveness is an insecure person's common reaction even to suggestions. Deeply rooted insecurity cannot take correction, because *all correction is perceived as rejection*. Therefore, you will never hear an insecure person with a controlling spirit admit to being wrong. It is always someone else's fault. Never is there confession of guilt, contrition or true remorse. If you confront a controller and insist on an apology, you will probably get a screaming response such as, "Yes, I'm wrong! I'm always wrong! I'm a total failure!" This sarcastic spewing is a long way from repentance. The loud volume of the sarcasm is the person's way of telling you, "I'm still in control."

Jesus' Abusive Situation

Jesus was in an abusive situation preceding Calvary, but in that time He committed Himself to His Father. He chose to entrust His life to the Father's hands, not take things into His own hands, "who, when He was reviled, did not revile in return; when He suffered, He did not threaten, but committed Himself to Him who judges righteously" (1 Peter 2:23).

Controllers do not want to leave things to God. They want to bring them to pass on their own. Not trusting God to vindicate them, they seek to control, justifying their actions as "doing it to others, before they do it to me."

The Holy Spirit is our Helper who strengthens us to overcome all obstacles. He teaches us to put our trust in God, not in ourselves, and leave the results to Him: "Behold, I lay in Zion, a chief cornerstone, elect, precious, and he who believes on Him will by no means be put to shame" (1 Peter 2:6).

In the next chapter, we will take a closer look at those whom controllers tend to gravitate toward and surround themselves with—people with an Ahab-like spirit of passivity. We will also find out more about why Jezebels and Ahabs often team up and form a working "agreement" with each other.

Questions to Consider

1. What are the three main ways a Jezebel spirit operates?
2. Why do people become controllers?
3. Name a few ways control takes root through insecurity.
4. What motivates controllers?

Prayer

Father God, I ask You to forgive me for any time I have used improper and controlling ways in my life. I repent of any pride and insecurity that have opened a door in my life to the operation of a Jezebel spirit. Like David, I pray, "Search me, O God, and know my heart; try me, and know my anxieties; and see if there is any wicked way in me, and lead me in the way everlasting" (Psalm 139:23–24). In Jesus' name, Amen.

8

Magnetic Attraction:
Ahabs and Jezebels

Bill was the pastor of a small but growing church in Texas. He admitted to me that he had always had an Ahab personality—passive, introverted and with far too willing an attitude to make everyone around him happy. As he was working hard to make his church grow, he also worked for a manufacturing company on the side. He expressed that he had always been a leader and would usually work as a foreman or superintendent. Yet at home he found himself disrespected by his wife, Brenda, and he had trouble making decisions and taking the leadership role.

Because of Brenda's domineering personality, Bill felt as though he was living in confusion. Even in situations where he knew he was right, he would concede and, in his words, "take the hit for her." Brenda would verbally abuse Bill, and then disrespect him for taking her abuse. On many occasions, following a church board meeting that he felt went well, she would chide him, accuse him of timidity and then override his authority. She constantly questioned his leadership and undermined him.

One day Brenda, after eighteen years of marriage, broke the news that she had been having an affair for quite some time. Bill had ignored all the signs, yet looking back, he saw that they were obvious. He still had trouble believing her, though, about her affair. She was unwilling to break off the relationship with this other man, and it was not long before they divorced. In the aftermath, Bill felt that the Lord told him to wait a few years before considering remarriage. His spiritual counselors advised the same thing.

Three years passed; then a woman named Sharon, with her four children in tow, came to church. She sat near the front and gave hearty nods and an amen of approval to everything Bill preached. She came for weeks and months, and finally they began to date. He told me that Sharon was everything he had ever hoped for in a woman and said they would talk about the Lord for hours and share Scriptures back and forth. Finally, after only three months of dating, they decided to get married.

The couple's honeymoon was not even over before Sharon told Bill that she had to have a cigarette. She indicated that she had kept her habit hidden, but she smoked several packs a day. She also loved to drink and was a borderline alcoholic. Sharon continued in her ways even though Bill held strong convictions against both her habits. Soon her violent temper also surfaced. She began making threats against Bill's reputation, using vile language and making up lies about his behavior. She would often tell him he was a terrible father to their children and a pathetic pastor.

When Bill and I met, he was beside himself with regret, not knowing what to do and kicking himself for getting into such a terrible predicament. Bill admitted that he had always been an Ahab with passive behavior, and now—although it seemed too late—he was ready to ask God for help and deliverance.

Truly he had found himself a second Jezebel for a wife, one who could be so sweet, subtle and nice and then turn on him with a vengeance, hurling accusations and verbal assaults. The only way Bill could clear his mind was to get away from Sharon. Ironically, she went to a deliverance team and told them enough lies about him that they got into agreement with her, telling her what she wanted to hear—that Bill was the Jezebel! They said *he* was the one who needed deliverance from that spirit.

Bill sought out godly counsel and was told to stand his ground. He was advised to stay very firm with Sharon until she genuinely repented. As of this writing, he has not yet seen a repentant heart in her, but thankfully he is no longer resorting to his Ahab-type behavior. Rather than being passive and taking the hits, Bill is standing strong.

Another man with an Ahab spirit was Pastor Roger, one of the kindest people you could ever meet. When he first began to pastor his church, people were excited. They were having wonderful times of worship and enjoying his preaching, and he was always seeking fresh revelation from the Lord. His wife, Sadie, however, although outwardly congenial, was very abrasive when dealing with individuals in the church—especially with those who were working hard to serve. She obviously had experienced severe childhood wounds that caused her to keep everyone in the church at arm's length.

Soon the church began to lose members—always, it seemed, for the same reason. Brutal in her approach with everyone, Sadie offended people. She also had a close friend, Mary, a very "mature" Jezebel whom she allowed to be in charge of the women's Bible studies and other church activities. Mary volunteered for everything and was a generous giver, but tragically, everyone Mary was involved with eventually left the church.

Pastor Roger either did not see or chose to ignore his wife's behavioral patterns in both the church and her relationship with Mary. Sadly, family after family left without telling him why. The situation was 1 Timothy 3:5 in action: "For if a man does not know how to rule his own house, how will he take care of the church of God?"

When someone finally told Pastor Roger what was behind so many members leaving, he became extremely defensive—probably feeling that confronting his wife would be too big a price to pay for changing things. Though a true man of God, he had given his authority away to his wife long ago. He refused to deal with her behavior or communicate that she would not be allowed to operate in such a manner. Without Pastor Roger stepping up to the plate, there was little hope for the church. Due to his Ahab-like passivity, the problems were never dealt with and the church finally fizzled down to just a few members.

Who Was Ahab?

We saw in chapter 1 that Ahab was the king of Israel who married Jezebel outside the will of God, relinquishing his power as king and husband to her. Just as Jezebel's name has become synonymous with a manipulative, controlling individual, Ahab's name has become synonymous with a passive individual who gives away his or her power.

Because of King Ahab's attitude toward Kingdom principles and the things of God, he left spiritual matters to his wife. Ahab even considered covenant marriage trivial. By marrying the daughter of a Sidonian king, he was looking for political power and money. It did not concern him that she was a pagan who encouraged sexual promiscuity and idolatry, and who surrounded herself with castrated men. Turning his back on God, Ahab served Baal and set up an altar in the temple he built for the false god:

> And it came to pass, as though it had been a *trivial* thing for him to walk in the sins of Jeroboam the son of Nebat, that he took as wife Jezebel the daughter of Ethbaal, king of the Sidonians;

and he went and served Baal and worshiped him. Then he set up an altar for Baal in the temple of Baal, which he had built in Samaria. And Ahab made a wooden image. Ahab did more to provoke the LORD God of Israel to anger than all the kings of Israel who were before him.

1 Kings 16:31–33, emphasis added

King Ahab let his wife lead him into a pagan religion instead of following the God of Israel. Consequently, he had the distinction of being called the most wicked king by God: "But there was no one like Ahab who sold himself to do wickedness in the sight of the LORD, because Jezebel his wife stirred him up" (1 Kings 21:25). Today, we give in to the same wicked spirit as King Ahab if we allow anything in our lives to require more of our focus and attention than we give to God. These things can be a "baal" that we worship.

Ahab was spineless. He quickly abdicated his authority to his wife and led Israel into idol worship. "He behaved very abominably in following idols, according to all that the Amorites had done, whom the LORD had cast out before the children of Israel" (1 Kings 21:26). He also abdicated his authority to her when he coveted Naboth's vineyard and let her do the dastardly deed of having the innocent man killed, as we talked about in chapter 1. She flattered her husband along the way, saying, "You now exercise authority over Israel! Arise, eat food, and let your heart be cheerful; I will give you the vineyard of Naboth the Jezreelite" (1 Kings 21:7). In reality, though, she was usurping his authority, and the whole incident strengthened her power over him. While Jezebel's preposterous action was despicable, Ahab was *just as guilty* as she was when he surrendered his rightful authority to her. How pleased God would have been if Ahab would have stood up to Jezebel's controlling, manipulative ways.

Like spineless King Ahab, Ahabs married to a Jezebel today may let their aggressive spouses take control in situations where they do not want to deal with something. And just like King Ahab, those with an Ahab spirit see the things of God as trivial. They often are not committed to following Kingdom principles when it comes to marriage, church attendance, proactive involvement in spiritual matters, taking the role of a leader with conviction, leading in prayer or teaching their children the Bible. An Ahab will leave it up to his or her spouse to decide where to attend church and will relinquish all other Kingdom decisions. Ahabs abdicate their power.

Defining the Ahab Spirit

Ahabs and Jezebels always seem to team up together. There is a kind of magnetic attraction between them. Because of their passivity, Ahabs enable and empower those with a propensity to control and dominate. An Ahab is usually fearful of being rebuked and can also be lazy and careless.

A man who is an Ahab has a distorted concept of his own authority, blames others (mainly his wife), justifies himself, leans on his wife, is a "mama's boy," is irresponsible and relinquishes authority over his house. Weak and childish, he pouts, is spoiled and throws temper tantrums. While many men are guilty of dominating their wives and families, a male with an Ahab spirit will cower before a spirit of control, fearing either an interruption of his sex life or verbal abuse (both illegitimate tools a controlling woman may use to get her way). Many men have succumbed to an Ahab spirit by refusing to lead their households in godly order. Sometimes they just do not care enough to take the lead.

A woman can also become an Ahab, especially if she is married to a man with a Jezebel spirit. Fearing a loss of financial security, she may become passive and surrender her authority and dignity in God to a controlling man. Whether male or female, those who have an Ahab spirit refuse to take their rightful place in God's call.

Nothing is more revolting than a passive, spineless person, especially a person who holds a position of authority such as a husband, pastor or elected official. It is appalling when an Ahab gives away authority to please or placate someone else, compromising his or her own beliefs and convictions in the process. How many times in politics have we seen elected officials compromise their convictions for their own advancement? Many of them fit into the Ahab category because they are people pleasers (peacekeepers, not peacemakers) who will not stand up to a Jezebel spirit.

On another occasion, King Ahab spared the life of King Ben-Hadad and, contrary to God's plan, made a deal with him instead of killing him (see 1 Kings 20). This was more behavior indicative of an Ahab spirit, which promotes a lazy passivity that is wicked in God's sight. In the parable of the talents, Jesus tells us about another man with an Ahab spirit, calling him wicked and lazy. A master gave his servants charge over some finances in his absence. When he returned, the man to whom he had given one talent returned it to him with no gain at all, not even interest. Everyone else oversaw their portions well and increased the master's money, but this servant had only excuses to offer. His laziness and inaction did not go over well with his master:

> He who had received the one talent came and said, "Lord, I knew you to be a hard man, reaping where you have not sown, and gathering where you have not scattered seed. And I was afraid, and went and hid your talent in the ground. Look, there you have what is yours."
>
> But his lord answered and said to him, "You *wicked and lazy* servant, you knew that I reap where I have not sown, and gather where I have not scattered seed. So you ought to have deposited

my money with the bankers, and at my coming I would have received back my own with interest. So take the talent from him, and give it to him who has ten talents."

Matthew 25:24–28, emphasis added

God will match our efforts, but He will not do our work. That would invade our free will. He wants us to be assertive and active—seeking and knocking on the door of life. Grace covers failure, but it will not make up for passivity.

What if we try and fail? That is called learning. Refusing to try is not learning; it is evil. There is no grace for that. We have to take responsibility for our lives. Philippians 2:12 instructs us, "Work out your own salvation with fear and trembling." And in Hebrews 10:38–39 the Lord says, "But if anyone draws back [premeditated withdrawal], My soul has no pleasure in him."

Ahabs Are Allies of Evil

Passivity is destructive to the soul and intolerable to God. Passive people are not evil, but those with Ahab-like passivity become allies of evil by not resisting or pushing against the active force of evil. The word *passive* means "nonacting" or "nonresisting." It comes from the Latin word meaning "to suffer." Some type of suffering is almost always the end result of passivity.

Passive people have become the way they are by giving up their identities. They will do almost anything to avoid the displeasure or disapproval of others. They also feel an intense need for acceptance and appreciation. They desperately want to be liked, and they literally (although usually subconsciously) will give up part or all of their identity and individuality just to make sure people will like them. When passive Ahabs are around controllers, they must come to a place of not giving up their identity.

Ahabs Are Peacekeepers, not Peacemakers

One of the best ways to describe a person bound with an Ahab spirit is as a peacekeeper. Ahabs hate confrontation and will do just about anything to avoid it and keep the peace. It is easy for them to live on the surface, look for immediate gratification and "find" peace by withdrawing from conflict. They might leave a room, walk away or even take on a time-consuming project as a means of escape. Sometimes Ahabs even escape unpleasantness by turning to drugs, alcohol or other types of addictions.

Ahabs want the temporary, immediate gratification of keeping the peace at any price. They do not want to go through the often confrontative process of "making peace" by boldly dealing with the issues at hand, which would result in more permanent, long-term gratification. Those caught in this Ahab passivity are also extremely slow to communicate their real feelings. This will cause any relationships to suffer and eventually collapse.

An Ahab husband is nonconfrontational to a fault. His emotional weakness enables a controlling wife to dominate him, because he lives in fear of her anger. He reasons that her anger will interrupt every aspect of his personal life, so he gives away his authority and surrenders to passivity. More and more he feels disrespected, and he concludes that he is not wanted or needed anymore. Due to his fear of failure and fear of confrontation, he gives up his right to lead the home. He also fears threats of public exposure of his weaknesses and will often retreat into silence—his way of maintaining what little control he still possesses.

Not every woman who lives with an Ahab husband is a Jezebel, by the way, even if she at first appears controlling. Some women with Ahab husbands are wrongly accused of being Jezebels because they have had no choice but to assume the authority and responsibility their passive husbands do not want. An Ahab husband puts inappropriate pressure on his wife because he does not want to deal with things. He will not help around the house or discipline the children. Between passivity and laziness, he figures that since he works all day, he can choose to be a couch potato after work. He forces his wife to make all the decisions that he should be making.

An Ahab-passive wife often is afraid to stand up to or disagree with her husband, so she blames herself for the way things are, telling herself that everything is her fault. Her dominating husband (who is spiritually weak and lacks the heart of a servant) intimidates her with his size and projected male hierarchy. He is not a leader, but a dictator. She may capitulate to passivity and stay in the marriage merely out of fear or for financial security.

Also, a woman with Ahab tendencies is sincere and wants strength, but she often will end up following a man who seems sensitive but turns out to be a manipulator. Such a wife ends up being offended by her husband because he does not lead her well or protect her, and she feels unloved. And rather than making healthy and assertive choices such as insisting on counseling, she eventually may lose all her self-esteem and shut down.

Ahabs Are Emotion Stuffers

Ahab personalities, male or female, do not deal well with their feelings. They develop a lifestyle of stuffing them. Bottled-up feelings do not just disappear; they affect every relationship an Ahab has. These stuffed emotions eventually turn into depression and anxiety, as well as passive-aggressive behaviors such as rage. As a result, Ahabs passively seek to manipulate others with the rage they feel inside. They might even outwardly displace anger onto others, especially those who love them. Passive behavior ultimately becomes passive-aggressive, and the mindset of a passive-aggressive person is, *I don't get mad—I get even.*

How Jezebels and Ahabs Relate

Both Ahabs and Jezebels are insecure and are looking outside themselves to find someone who will complement and enable them. Those with a Jezebel spirit are wounded; they have rejection issues and cannot tolerate being wrong. They are looking for acceptance through power and recognition. It is all about them! Their attitude is, *You are in this world to make me happy—and if you do not, there will be the devil to pay.*

Those with an Ahab spirit have unworthiness and inferiority issues. They are looking for love, acceptance and affirmation. They actually can be just as selfish, controlling and even manipulative as Jezebels—in a passive-aggressive way—because they give their power away to get love in return. Their actions are just as wrong as a Jezebel's.

Jezebels and Ahabs each take on a role God did not intend in an attempt to gain wholeness through a means other than God. Let's take a closer look at the magnetic relationship between them and see how they depend on each other in some very unhealthy ways.

Ahabs and Jezebels Cannot Exist without Each Other

Ahabs and Jezebels live in an unholy alliance. Whether it is in marriage, a family or church, they have an ungodly relationship. In one sense the two hate one another, but in another sense they feed off each other. They enable one another in order to get what they want. They always seem to team up together because of their "need" for one another.

Jezebels are looking for someone to control in order to carry out their agenda, and Ahabs are looking for someone to affirm their identity. Theirs is a love-hate relationship, and it is always abusive. When you see an Ahab or a Jezebel, you will always find the other half waiting in the wings somewhere. What makes their alliance unholy is that God is not involved. Their dependency is not on God but on each other. Their dysfunction opposes the way God created us.

Ahabs Are Martyrs; Jezebels Are Narcissists

Ahabs come across as selfless, but their innate selfishness is just more hidden so they will look good to others. They live like victims or martyrs. The ultimate Ahabs draw all the attention to themselves, and they often stay in a marriage because of the children. They manage early on to get the children to volunteer as their emotional support system, which is extremely unhealthy. Ahabs allow their partners to take advantage of them (appearing selfless), then they draw the children into taking sides.

Ahabs also consciously give their power away in order to get another person to validate their identities and tell them who they are. They think, *If I love you enough, you will love me,* and they look for partners who will tell them they are worthy and lovable. However, it flies in the face of God for a passive person to give someone else the power to tell them they are worthy. Worth comes from God alone and from being created in His image. No person can take away someone else's identity in Christ, yet Ahabs usually attack their own identities, believing whatever Jezebels say to them.

Jezebels are extremely narcissistic and self-serving. Because of their previous wounds stemming from abuse and rejection, they live with a defensive, self-protective, strike-first mentality. They also live without concern for the damage they cause others. The world is all about them, and from their perspective, the world is here to serve them.

Jezebels will always seek to get their needs met in an unhealthy way. They usually have such low self-worth that they need to partner with someone passive who believes that he or she is a bad person. That is why Jezebel and Ahab personalities always seem to end up together. A Jezebel (male or female) will find a passive Ahab match (male or female) who is looking for identity so much that he or she will almost "welcome" the abuse inherent in such a relationship.

Ahabs Are More Willing to Change than Jezebels

Jezebels are very unwilling to change. They hate change and resist it. Ahabs are almost always the ones to seek help and to change because they are looking for connection. Counselors say that these passive personalities will come for help because of their desperate need for intimacy. They often are connected to Jezebels with ambivalent, or cold-to-warm personalities—warm when they need something and cold when they have what they desire. This combination of an intimacy-starved Ahab and an ambivalent Jezebel makes for ongoing marital difficulties. Marriage was meant to be celebrated. Couples can be healed so that they celebrate their differences rather than being in continual conflict. We need to live where we are celebrated, not where we are tolerated!

At the Root of Passivity

Is passivity a demonic influence? Is it simply a personality trait? Is it laziness or spiritual weakness clothed in the fear of asserting oneself? It can be all of the above. Passivity has its roots in demonic blindness, where Satan assaults people's self-worth to the point that it suffocates their ability to stand up for themselves and confront situations and conflicts. This blindness paralyzes individuals to the extent that they choose not to say or do anything.

Passivity can also come from an inherited personality trait "modeled" by a parent and other significant people. My passive mother "taught" me passivity, for example.

But most importantly, I believe that passivity is a spiritual problem stemming from the fear of man; a self-abasement

141

scenario of not caring enough to embrace one's own dignity as a redeemed human being. This comes not from a redeemed human spirit, but rather from a soul in need of restoration in the mind, will and emotions.

If you want to delve more into the problem of Ahab-like passivity and what to do about it, my book *Discerning and Defeating the Ahab Spirit* will help. There you will find more information on passive versus aggressive behavior, dealing with woundedness and lifelong patterns, and living assertively through Jesus Christ so that you can enjoy the freedom that kind of healthy spiritual lifestyle brings. But for now, since we have just seen what the "opposite" of Jezebel looks like in those with Ahab-like, passive tendencies, let's return to the subject of Jezebel and learn a few more things about how someone with that spirit strives to take control.

Questions to Consider

1. Describe some of the defining characteristics of those with an Ahab spirit.
2. Define passivity. Do you see any passive traits in yourself?
3. Why do Jezebels and Ahabs usually end up in relationships with one another?

Prayer

Lord God, I ask You to deliver me from an Ahab spirit. Forgive me for the times that I have lived passively, tolerating evil and not standing strong for the truth. Forgive me for treating Your Kingdom principles as trivial, and help me to become a peacemaker, not a peacekeeper. In Jesus' name, Amen.

9

Eyes Wide Open

Nathan had his initial experience with a spirit of control in his first pastorate. He had accepted an invitation to pastor a group of people who had begun meeting in a home in a popular and growing Florida city. Upon arriving in the city as the "new pastor," he was informed that a neighboring pastor overseeing the group had done him the "favor" of appointing a woman to be in charge of the bookkeeping until he and his family had officially begun pastoring the new church. This woman had a classic spirit of control, which became evident in Nathan's first few days in the city. This put him in an extremely awkward situation. Being only faintly acquainted with his new congregation, he was unable to replace the woman immediately without stirring up a lot of trouble.

Increasingly, Nathan became aware that there was a problem when he discovered that the woman had begun seeking housing for his family—without his or his wife's consent. Housing, of course, was something they needed very much, but her motive did not involve meeting their needs, but rather her own. This became more evident with each encounter. She wanted to be involved in every decision concerning the church. She craved power and recognition.

The bookkeeper's husband was a typical Ahab with a passive nature. He had become weary of combating her incredible drive to be involved in everyone's life, so he had totally abdicated his authority to her and buried himself in his work. He chose to turn a blind eye to the way she had usurped his authority, and he obviously had lost all hope of her changing.

As is typical of a Jezebel, this woman was exuberantly helpful, volunteering for everything—almost to the point of replacing the need for anyone else at any time. There was no question that she wanted to be at the center of everything and privy to information that was none of her business. She was a classic example of how those under a Jezebel spirit seek position and power and will pay just about any price for them. Although Nathan was a young and inexperienced pastor, he was aware that her pushiness was inappropriate. Her behavior made him more and more uncomfortable.

The Element of Surprise

The most eye-opening experience Nathan had concerning the woman's Jezebel spirit occurred just a few days after he and his wife arrived in town. The local pastor who had been overseeing things agreed to give him some insight and guidance in getting the church off the ground, and they arranged a meeting to discuss things. Nathan was eager to get this pastor's advice and input and was looking forward to their private meeting at his new apartment. After the local pastor arrived, they exchanged pleasantries and began to discuss possible strategies for the new church. It seemed only minutes had passed when there was a sudden knock at the door. To Nathan's amazement, it was this bookkeeper! She explained that she was "feeling a leading" to drop by.

As always seems to happen with a Jezebel, she totally caught him off guard, blindsiding him. First of all, this was a private meeting between the pastors that this woman had no business attending. Secondly, she boldly invited herself and stayed for over two hours. Lastly, and most significantly, she quickly began interjecting her unsolicited thoughts and desires for the newly born church into the discussion.

Looking back, Nathan realized that he should have insisted that she leave, as it was a private meeting. But as a young pastor unsure about how to fully exert his authority, he let her stay. He was appalled at her gall and amazed that she had the audacity to intrude on the meeting. He was also angry at himself for not standing up to her. But even then, he knew that asking her to leave would cause an ugly confrontation.

This type of intrusiveness is so typical of a Jezebel. Through the years I have learned, as Nathan did, how those with a Jezebel spirit use the element of surprise. They specialize in catching you off guard in order to strengthen their foothold and increase their power and influence in the circumstances surrounding their involvement.

Rooting Out Jezebel

As I mentioned in chapter 5, Jezebels are usually extremely clairvoyant. This woman "knew" of this important meeting (with the assistance of a familiar spirit) and wanted to be on the inside. She also controlled things in many other ways. For example, as church bookkeeper, one of her duties was to prepare Nathan's paycheck. Each time his salary came due, however, she would dangle the check out in front of him, as if she were the source of the money and was paying it out of her own resources. This, too, caught him off guard. He later stated in retrospect that he should have trusted his instincts and declared her behavior unacceptable, informing her that she was not his source. He should have refused to let her gloat altogether and insisted that she leave his check in a designated place.

Although the bookkeeper's arrogant handling of the pastor's rightful compensation may seem like a small thing, it revealed only the tip of the iceberg when it came to her controlling and manipulative personality. Confrontation is really the only "cure" in dealing with such a Jezebel spirit. The problem is that many leaders fear confrontation, knowing it will create an ugly scene. Therefore, they prolong the inevitable. When weeds are pulled early in the spring, they come out easily, but if you wait a few weeks, their root system gets established and they are much more difficult to remove. So it is with a controlling person's roots, which only go down deeper the longer the person's behavior goes unchecked. The results taint more and more lives, until the person is ultimately confronted.

Through prayer, things eventually came to a head with Nathan and the bookkeeper. He caught her in several inconsistencies. He did not handle things with the greatest of wisdom, and things went from bad to worse. When he relieved her of her duties, he tried to show love and handle things professionally, but the trouble had already begun. Jezebel already had a foothold and was well networked in the church.

Jezebels do not release power easily. The woman immediately began to draw sympathy from her family and all those in the church whom she had already craftily intertwined into her life. It was amazing how she had sown damaging seed into so many lives. She skillfully portrayed herself as the innocent person who had been betrayed. Taking on the spirit of a martyr, she quickly enlisted many in her "cause."

In churches and other Christian organizations, people with a Jezebel spirit often hold positions of influence. Many times, they are appointed to serve in a spiritual position because they are influential in the business world or in their profession. Appointing them on this basis can be deadly because their flesh is uncrucified and their will is unbroken before Christ. It is like putting an immature child in charge of a corporation. This puts a tourniquet around the potential flow of the Holy Spirit and thereby the fruitfulness of the church or Christian group involved.

Jezebels have usually worked their way up in an organization or church, and because no one has confronted them along the way, they are seemingly immovable. Some have served in a position of power for so many years that their names (in a very negative sense) are synonymous with the place itself. As a guest speaker invited to such places, I can feel a spirit of control operating in the atmosphere and trying to intimidate me. Discerning Christians who potentially could have been a blessing to such an organization or church have not joined, knowing it is under the influence of a strong Jezebel personality (male or female), not of the Holy Spirit.

Although we love those in the grip of a Jezebel spirit, we cannot sympathize with them or tolerate their controlling behavior. The Holy Spirit must be in charge, and we must have leaders who fear God and do not have a people-pleasing spirit. God is raising up leaders who, like David, have a heart after God Himself. They have no agenda and no need for recognition. They desire only to be an instrument of blessing for the increase of God's Kingdom. God is also raising up Elijahs who have no fear of Jezebel.

Three Types of Love

> But if you have bitter envy and self-seeking in your hearts, do not boast and lie against the truth. This wisdom does not descend from above, but is earthly, sensual, demonic. For where envy and self-seeking exist, confusion and every evil thing will be there.

> But the wisdom that is from above is first pure, then peaceable, gentle, willing to yield, full of mercy and good fruits, without partiality and without hypocrisy.
>
> James 3:14–17

People who operate with a Jezebel spirit usually have twisted thinking where love and authority are concerned. In fact, one of the most deceptive characteristics about Jezebels is the manner in which they "love" a person whom they are using for the wrong motives. The world does not function in agape (divine) love, but only in eros love that asks, "What's in it for me?" Have you ever watched an actor or professional musician say "I love you" to a huge crowd after winning an award? What they love is the adulation and the feeling that they are on top of the world. How can you love someone you do not even know?

When controllers say they love you, it is also insincere. Their "love" is not a divine agape love or even a refined human love. Rather, it is a totally selfish love with its own agenda, seeking recognition or control. When confronted or rejected, that twisted love is anything but divine. Its selfishness and self-seeking will be revealed if you disagree with Jezebels or confront them about an issue. They will call you names and threaten to destroy you. Beware once you cross or confront a Jezebel spirit. This person who "loved" you more than life itself will now turn on you. The same power that loved you now turns into an equal power devoted to destroying you and your reputation. The Jezebel, although his or her motive was twisted, now feels scorned and betrayed and will go to *any* length to hurt you. Confidences you made will now be used as weapons against you. Like Elijah running from Jezebel, you feel like running for cover, the intimidation of that spirit is so powerful.

Manipulative love (eros) says, "I'll do something for you if you do something for me." There are self-seeking motives and strings attached to this kind of love. It is "love with a hook," as Bible teacher Bob Mumford says. Sadly, many are unaware of it when they are being manipulated. Manipulation is nothing more than actions someone performs to get you to agree and conform to this "lover's" wishes. Basically, you are being used. Flattery is also in a controller's toolbox: "For there is no faithfulness in their mouth; their inward part is destruction; their throat is an open tomb; they flatter with their tongue" (Psalm 5:9).

Possessive love is a suffocating expression of love, and total devotion is expected in return. Jezebels are not only demanding, but consuming of your time and attention. We saw this in chapter 4's story of the graduate student dating a possessive Jezebel. If you do not allow such people to possess you, or if you dare give your attention to someone or something other than them, they will turn on you with a vengeance. Their mentality is that they own you. They have done you favors in order to put you in their debt. You have the devil to pay if you do not reciprocate and let them treat you like a puppet.

Divine love gives and expects nothing in return—no strings attached. Divine love leaves you totally free to make your own decisions. Jesus Christ is the perfect expression of divine love. Naturally, God desires that Christians mature into His divine love, abandoning selfish gain, motives and ambitions.

Ammunition for Jezebel

Jezebels continually collect ammunition. By this I mean they collect information! They are all about finding out anything they can about your past or about any offense involving you and others. In their minds, this is information they can use against you if they ever begin to lose their grip on you. Anything you confide to a controlling person can and will be used against you later—without mercy.

I have talked with many people who have confided something personal to a Jezebel, thinking it would never be repeated. It did not take long for them to find out differently. Because controllers are insecure and cannot tolerate rejection, if you should ever contradict their desires, you will find out differently, too. The information they have collected about you serves as ammunition for the purpose of retaliation. If you threaten their power and influence or try to pull away from them, they will seek to destroy you.

It is difficult to comprehend the "spiritual" power a Jezebel possesses. In the previous example about the bookkeeper, Nathan told me how he would catch himself offering personal information whenever they had a conversation. To his dismay, he would realize later that he had confided way too much and that the information he had "surrendered" likely would be used against him. When Nathan told her things, he would instinctively know that they were none of her business. He could not understand why he even was offering her information in the first place. The more information he gave her, especially personal information, the more vulnerable it left him to the wiles of Jezebel.

As I mentioned before, something about the deceiving power of a Jezebel spirit seems to pull conversation out of you and makes you feel that you almost owe a person information. But when the person is exposed, *you* will become the target of this armed Jezebel who has milked you for the information. A Jezebel will twist this knowledge to his or her advantage in an attempt to gain the upper hand so that you are made to look the "fool," and he or she is the "righteous one." Only by refusing to back down and countering all accusations with the truth will you be able to stand.

Stealing My Microphone

During my first year and a half serving as a pastor, I was invited to speak in Arizona. The day before I was scheduled to return home, I had a dream in which I was standing behind the pulpit at our church and a number of people stood around me, all grasping for my microphone. It erupted into a scuffle until I stood alone holding the microphone, with loose and disconnected wires dangling from it. Then a friend of mine who is greatly used by God in the gift of prophecy stepped forward and spoke something to the effect that God was going to take charge of the situation. Next, as I was still standing with the microphone, about thirty disgruntled people stood up and walked out of the back of the church. Then almost instantly, sixty or seventy people came in, more than doubling those who had left. Then the dream ended.

I flew home the following day. When I arrived at the Sunday morning service, something obviously was amiss. Although I was the pastor, I did not feel welcome. The next two days were like a whirlwind. Many things came to the surface, revealing jealousy and various factions among the people. I was accused of being everything from a one-man show to a false prophet to possibly the Antichrist. The venom directed at me made no sense.

Looking back, I realized that from the inception of the church, a large number of people had come with their own agendas, seeking position and power. When I was slow to appoint them to any position they desired, their jealousy and opposition escalated, finally coming to a head while we were away in Arizona on a ministry trip.

In the days following my return, I sought counsel from my pastor in Kansas City, as well as from many other ministers to whom I looked for spiritual direction and guidance. They all gave me similar wisdom and godly counsel.

Confrontation Time

When I returned to the pulpit on Sunday, I felt led not to preach, but instead to deal with the situation. I began by making a confession. "I don't know how to pastor a church," I admitted.

When I spoke those words, sighs of relief filled the auditorium. Then I continued, "But neither do you know how to pastor a church; only the Holy Spirit does."

If they were unprepared for the first statement, they surely were even more unprepared for the second.

I spent the next thirty minutes exposing all the hearsay and clearing the air of all the gossip that had come to my ears. I did not want the devil to have any darkness in which to function. "God is light and in Him is no darkness at all" (1 John 1:5). Then I restated our vision and purpose and made a point of not apologizing for the fact that God had called me to pastor that church. That day I lost thirty people, coinciding with the prophetic dream God had given me. But exactly as in the dream, we gained seventy more people (more than twice the number we had lost) by the following Sunday.

From that point, we began to grow as a church. God's wisdom had gathered all the poison together and then purged it all at once. All those striving for control were now removed. Although we were not without difficulties, an atmosphere of health filled the church, and the presence of God was manifest in a fresher and greater dimension.

The principle I learned was the one Jesus put into words in John 15:2: "Every branch in Me that does not bear fruit He takes away; and every branch that bears fruit He prunes, that it may bear more fruit." It is true of both people and organizations.

God's Church

In another portion of the same dream, God was correcting me. As I stood before the people (right before the struggle began for my microphone), my pockets appeared to be bulging with paraphernalia. Various items were hanging out everywhere. It looked ridiculous. Then in very distinct letters in front of me was the word *preoccupied*.

In this part of the dream, God was clearly rebuking me. Along with indicating how He would deal with the spirit of control, He also was telling me to get my priorities straight as a pastor.

During those following weeks, I not only repented of being preoccupied, but I took action to set my life in order. Like many pastors, I was absorbed with far too many insignificant details. As the Holy Spirit specifically pointed out, I was distracted and preoccupied. Jesus Christ is the head of the Church (see Ephesians 1:22), and He corrects leadership as well as the entire Body of Christ.

Two Sides

There are always two sides to the same coin. Many times leaders think they are exempt from correction. While God is setting things in order, He will correct leadership as well as those who are rebellious against authority. It is of utmost importance that leaders remain teachable and have the heart of a servant, not a tyrant.

In leadership, ego probably stands in the way more than any other factor. When ego is not dealt with, leaders begin to think of themselves as flawless and faultless. Jesus is our example, and He opposes the proud: "God resists the proud, but gives grace to the humble" (1 Peter 5:5).

Some of the most blatant acts of control I have ever seen have emanated from the pulpit. Control through manipulation, intimidation and fear has been used to trap people in a church or in an abusive situation, which is an illegitimate use of divine authority. A leader must be a broken vessel, one whose will is surrendered to God so that he stands in God's authority, not his own. Unbroken vessels tend to dominate people in order to keep them under control for the sake of their own agenda. When

God breaks the will, a leader can legitimately stand in God's authority, because he or she is *under* His authority.

There is no greater freedom than being under God's authority. We are free from having to defend ourselves and from seeking our own agendas. We know that we have no rights, because Jesus has purchased our lives with His own blood. We stand free to serve. God is an awesome master, and He knows how to take care of His own.

In the next chapter, we will examine more closely what happens in leadership situations when a spirit of Jezebel manifests through those in authority over others.

Questions to Consider

1. Why do Jezebels want information from you?
2. Which of the three types of love do those with a Jezebel spirit operate in? Why?
3. Why is it so important for leaders to be broken vessels?

Prayer

Father God, I ask You to give me discernment regarding any type of control in me or others. Open my eyes to anything coming from a wrong motive, and give me the boldness and authority to confront inappropriate behavior sooner rather than later. Help me to flow in Your agape love, and deliver me from selfishness and self-centered living. Help me to be a broken vessel before You so that I can stand in Your authority, not my own. In Jesus' name, Amen.

10

How Jezebels Abuse Authority

For several consecutive years, I was invited as a guest speaker at a nondenominational church in the southern United States. It always struck me as unusual that the attendance in every service was exactly the same. If four hundred were present Sunday morning, four hundred would be present Sunday evening . . . and Monday evening, and Tuesday. At first I interpreted this as faithfulness on the part of everyone, but later it became evident that the pastor had taught submission to authority to such an extreme that people were too fearful to ever miss a meeting. It was not allowed.

Later, I learned that people were not only instructed never to miss a meeting, but they also were instructed not to take vacations unless they coincided appropriately with the church schedule. Neither was anyone allowed to question any of the teaching, the finances or church operations. If they did, they were disciplined for being in rebellion. The pastor, who seemed so kind on the surface, was Hitler-like in his dominion over the people. After a few years, things began to unravel there. Those who had lived under such fear and control began to be set free, and the pastor was eventually exposed for immorality.

Looking back, I recall now how the church had an undeniably intimidating and oppressive atmosphere. It was difficult to speak freely and experience the flow of the Holy Spirit there.

Some leaders are very number-conscious and are unable to "keep" people solely with the presence of God, so they resort to fear and bondage. They make statements like, "If you leave this church, you will be without a spiritual covering." This is often effective because it wraps people in a spirit of fear. Submission to authority is frequently used as an argument to keep from losing members. Although it is a scriptural principle, it can become legalism and produce bondage, not freedom. Anything preached through a legalistic mindset produces death, "For the letter kills, but the Spirit gives life" (2 Corinthians 3:6). Any time people preach submission to authority, loyalty and commitment without basing those on the foundation of love, it will produce robot-like believers bound by fear. But fear should *never* motivate a believer, only love and the motivation to please and obey God.

Leadership is about service, not self-preservation or personal advancement. The heart of a servant must be priority one. Peter defined a shepherd's job description this way:

> Tend (nurture, guard, guide, and fold) the flock of God that is [your responsibility], not by coercion or constraint, but willingly; not dishonorably motivated by the advantages and profits [belonging to the office], but eagerly and cheerfully; not domineering [as arrogant, dictatorial, and overbearing persons] over those in your charge, but being examples (patterns and models of Christian living) to the flock (the congregation). And [then] when the Chief Shepherd is revealed, you will win the conqueror's crown of glory.
>
> 1 Peter 5:2–4, AMP

God is watching over those who watch over His flock. Look at His rebuke to shepherds in Ezekiel 34:2–4:

> Thus says the Lord GOD to the shepherds: "Woe to the shepherds of Israel who feed themselves! Should not the shepherds feed the flocks? You eat the fat and clothe yourselves with the wool; you slaughter the fatlings, but you do not feed the flock. The weak you have not strengthened, nor have you healed those who were sick, nor bound up the broken, nor brought back what was driven away, nor sought what was lost; but with force and cruelty you have ruled them."

Submitting to godly authority is vital, but so is avoiding those who abuse authority. On the one hand, we need to have a teachable and submissive spirit. On the other hand, we need to be discerning and have zero tolerance for those who abuse an office, possibly under a Jezebel spirit, and use it for their personal gain.

Using Fear and Bondage

The first time I heard Pastor Charles preach, the Holy Spirit clearly spoke to me the name *Gestapo*. At first I brushed it off, thinking that the pastor seemed like a nice guy. But before long, I saw the pattern that is always evident in someone with a Jezebel spirit. This pastor's extreme insecurity became more and more obvious as I sensed his iron-handed control over the people. He manipulated them continually, promoting himself by insisting that his congregation bless and honor him because he was "good ground." Some in the congregation told me they felt more like prisoners than worshipers. He continually made public statements such as, "If you ever leave this church, you are missing God," and "Don't touch God's anointed," which implied that you could never disagree with him or question anything he said.

The most common weakness in those serving as leaders is insecurity. Insecure leaders like Pastor Charles are easily threatened by anyone who could potentially question their position or authority. As a result, they overcompensate in taking action to keep people in the grip of their control. They also become authoritarian and obstinate in dominating a church. These types will often refuse accountability and become critical of all other leadership, isolating themselves from fellowship. And as Proverbs 18:1 points out, "A man who isolates himself seeks his own desire."

Typically, those with controlling tendencies also show no genuine freedom and specifically no joy—hardly a smile. It seems as if their only joy is being in control. When the Holy Spirit is in control, however, the freedom and joy everyone experiences is priceless and hard to explain. You can make a mistake without being fearful or just plain enjoy the presence of the Lord. "Now the Lord is the Spirit; and where the Spirit of the Lord is, there is liberty" (2 Corinthians 3:17).

Pastor Charles also displayed other control issues. He would not tolerate any marital problems in the church because it hurt the church's image. When married couples had unresolved conflicts, he always sided with the woman and harshly stood against the husband, till the husband had no choice but to leave. Pastor Charles also had his own group of friends who surrounded him. Interestingly, it seemed more than coincidental that they all had abundant finances and frequently bought him gifts, took him on hunting and fishing expeditions and flew him different places. When he accepted speaking engagements, he insisted on flying first-class and would not consider riding coach—he was a man of God and "deserved the best."

Verbally, Pastor Charles said he wanted the gifts of the Spirit to operate in the church, but he gave absolutely no opportunity for anyone to operate freely in the gifts. The only person who could function in that way was him. If anyone ever did step out with a prophetic utterance, they would be "corrected."

Things began to fall apart at the church when Pastor Charles appointed his son as the youth leader. Although his son was married, he had sexual encounters with two girls in the youth group who were only fifteen. As Pastor Charles had done with other family members and close friends, he swept this under the rug and refused to make his son deal with the consequences. He excused the sin, saying it was not really sin, just a problem with his son's flesh. Remember what happened to Eli when he refused to deal with his sons who were committing sexual acts of immorality in the Temple? God judged him: "For I have told him that I will judge his house forever for the iniquity which he knows, because his sons made themselves vile, and he did not restrain them" (1 Samuel 3:13).

Tactics of a Controlling Leader

One way leaders with a Jezebel spirit operate is to label anyone who does not submit to their authority as rebellious. Certainly some people are rebellious and will not submit to godly authority. But good people also resent being controlled. For example, people may be wise not to submit to leadership under which the Holy Spirit is quenched time after time, the people are manipulated into giving an offering and the pastor uses the pulpit to vent his "side" of an issue without giving the people an opportunity to think for themselves.

People also feel violated when scathing sermons are preached that are obvious attacks against individual members. When a pastor wants to deal with someone he feels is "out of line," for instance, his sermon might revolve around the rebellion of Korah (see Numbers 16). That in itself is out of line. If a pastor is secure in God, he can confront any rebellion in a called meeting and give people a chance to vent their concerns and disappointments. Anything else is cowardly and shows improper etiquette and protocol.

Another manipulative tactic of controlling leaders is to build their own kingdoms and bring increase to their ranks without waiting on God to add to the church. The Holy Spirit is well able to speak to individuals regarding the church He wants them to belong to, but these leaders do not want to wait on that process. They give newcomers an instant title; visitors to their churches are approached almost immediately and given a job. The naïve and innocent quickly succumb to the temptation of wearing a title, thinking, *Finally, a place that needs me*. But they are only victims sucked in to add to the numbers. Once they have a job title (menial though it may be), they feel obligated to stay and "serve," so the church has accomplished its task and just added a new member.

Though this is done illegitimately, the leader does not care since the main thing is "building the business" and accumulating clients. In God's eyes, perhaps what these leaders are doing is running a business—one that has nothing to do with building His Church. Building a religious organization with a religious name does not always build His Kingdom. As God said to the church at Sardis, "You have a name that you are alive, but you are dead" (Revelation 3:1).

How Does God Count Growth?

People count growth by looking at things outwardly and counting the number of warm bodies filling large buildings. God does not count that way! God counts growth in the maturing of individual Christians. It is the difference between building organizations and building people. Good leaders focus on building people. When individuals are growing in their relationship with the Lord, learning to hear from God and yielding up their carnal thoughts to receive God's thoughts, the Church is growing. The number of people who pack buildings—who are often coerced into becoming part of a growing organization called a "church"—does not necessarily have anything to do with increasing the Kingdom of God. Sometimes a "successful" church numerically has sacrificed its potential intimacy with God for a more crowd-pleasing, seeker-sensitive format. Above all, the Lord desires an atmosphere where the Holy Spirit is allowed to move freely. When He is in charge, He meets the needs of people.

I have heard well-known ministers state publicly that if a church does not show enormous megagrowth, it does not have God's blessing. To the contrary, the opposite may be true. First of all, not every church is destined to be large, any more than every family is destined to be large. While carnal people measure only numbers, many smaller churches have value far beyond the attendance count. These small churches raise up quality ministries and send them forth, and they often have a huge outreach, letting God use them as funnels to distribute His provision to needy places.

Many Christian groups have paid a high price for the vision God has given them. Multitudes do not exactly flock to places where the Holy Spirit has required that people pay the high price of giving up their self-will. Jesus spent a lot of time investing Himself in only twelve disciples. Most cities of any size have elementary schools, high schools, colleges and graduate schools. Perhaps churches are the same way—some serve as elementary schools, some as high schools and some as colleges or graduate schools when it comes to maturing in Christ. The higher you go, the greater the price there is to pay—just as in the natural world.

God measures Kingdom increase by looking at the increase in people's spiritual lives, not by counting how many believers are med into one building. Churches that are large in number consist of those who refuse to mature spiritually. We all love to see expansion, and numerical growth is wonderful—as long as God brings the increase.

Only God Calls People

Godly leaders ought not get ahead of God in appointing people to positions in the church. Their part is to watch what God is doing—in effect, to watch the cream rise to the top. As God puts His approval and anointing on someone, the leaders can recognize this and agree with God.

Sadly, many church elders are selected by men, not chosen and appointed by God. Because man judges outwardly, a carnally minded pastor may choose elders on the basis of their business skills, their professional success, their popularity, prestige or friendliness. He may neglect to take into account the most vital ingredient—their spiritual maturity and development. Are they yielded and humble before God, or are they spiritual toddlers? The problem with baby Christians is that they come in adult bodies. If the spiritually immature are appointed to leadership positions, they will cause much heartache.

Naturally, a pastor might appoint deacons, ushers and church workers, but no man can appoint an elder or call someone into ministry—only God can. A true elder should be an extension of the pastoral leadership, capable of hearing God and able to preach and teach. His character should be one of stability, loyalty and faithfulness (see 1 Timothy 3:1–7). Neither should anyone strive for the five-fold ministry of an apostle, prophet, evangelist, pastor or teacher (see Ephesians 4:11). Either people are called of God, or they are not. May God deliver us from titles, which are often only for recognition by man.

Ego and a Love of Money

Ben Franklin reportedly said, "Nine out of ten men can handle failure, but only one out of ten can handle success." Unfortunately, there are some pastors who are excellent teachers and preachers of the Word of God, but much of their gift is eclipsed by their egos. Rather than seeing themselves as servants whom God has called to lay down their lives for the sheep, they see themselves as chief executive officers of a large company. They boss people around, running their churches like a business rather than part of the Kingdom of God. To say the least, humility is greatly needed in the pastorate. A pastor should be accessible and approachable, not egotistical. Nothing gets in God's way more than ego. A great acronym for ego is *Easing God Out.*

It is God who gives those in the office of a pastor legitimate authority. A pastor should not have to apologize for the position to which God has called him. He should not have to ask the church board for permission to invite a certain guest ministry or seek permission from a committee to make a minor purchase for the church. However, neither should he abuse his power and position. Some pastors who never had much success financially prior to being called into the ministry have no problem spending the church's money extravagantly. These pastors have no trouble using church finances for excessive lunches and luxury items. Some never had a decent automobile before their pastoral appointment, but they are not reluctant to trade cars every year as pastors, freely squandering their churches' money. Recently a group of people approached me regarding their pastor, who had purchased five new cars in the last three years—totally at the expense of the church.

Egotistical pastors protect their egos. They become unapproachable and label anyone who questions their abuse of finances as opposition from the devil. They live extravagant lifestyles while their churches are hurting, and they may preach that struggling people do not have their kind of faith. A true leader, on the other hand, loves the sheep and does not use them to gain a better life for himself.

If you disagree with controlling pastors at any level, you will hear "touch not God's anointed" (see Psalm 105:15). You cannot make any decisions outside their influence—only they "hear from God." These controllers will constantly remind you that they are your source of spiritual enlightenment. They proclaim that you are being trained, but because of their insecurity, they will never release you into ministry out from under their thumb. To keep you there, you are told that if you leave their churches, God will judge you and disaster will strike.

Pauper Pastors

This is not to say that the opposite never happens—instead of a pastor abusing a church's finances, a church sometimes abuses a pastor financially. Those with a poverty spirit love to control leadership by refusing to bless them financially. That is also wrong. In countless churches, congregations keep their pastors as paupers, never treating them with respect as laborers worthy of their hire. Deacons and elders under a spirit of control use manipulation to "keep the pastor humble." Some balk at every leader who dares to move ahead with a vision, not acknowledging that the vision God gives a pastor will require both some risk taking and some financial backing.

If we are generous and bless our leaders, God will bless us accordingly. We are to honor those who labor among us:

> Let the elders who rule well be counted worthy of double honor, especially those who labor in the word and doctrine. For the Scripture says, "You shall not muzzle an ox while it treads out the grain," and, "The laborer is worthy of his wages."
>
> 1 Timothy 5:17–18

Remember those who rule over you, who have spoken the word of God to you, whose faith follow, considering the outcome of their conduct.

Hebrews 13:7

Obey those who rule over you, and be submissive, for they watch out for your souls, as those who must give account. Let them do so with joy and not with grief, for that would be unprofitable for you.

Hebrews 13:17

God is generous. He lavishes blessings on people, even those whom we consider the most undeserving, but He resists the proud (see 1 Peter 5:5). Godly leaders know the difference between authority and arrogance. They understand that respect must be earned, and they know that God-given authority must be accompanied by humility, compassion and a servant's heart. They are careful to follow these words of Jesus:

You know that the rulers of the Gentiles lord it over them, and those who are great exercise authority over them. Yet it shall not be so among you; but whoever *desires to become great among you, let him be your servant.*

Matthew 20:25–26, emphasis added

We should honor such pastors and leaders among us and make sure that we are never a party to abusing them or treating them with disrespect financially or in other ways.

It is not uncommon, by the way, for the abuse of a leader to have much more far-reaching effects than we might anticipate. A pastor who, in his younger years, watched a father or other relative suffer abuse from a church board and body is very likely to become a controlling leader himself. As a result of his early wounds, he will tend to brace himself against similar abuse. He may go into a pastorate attempting to control others before they can control him. When self-preservation is the goal, his insecurity will demand respect and honor he has not yet earned. That sets up a difficult scenario right from the start.

Basically a Liar

In the rest of this chapter, I want to provide you with other examples of the abuses I have witnessed in leadership situations. Learning about my experiences may help you be discerning in a situation you face so that you do not become subject to an abusive leader. Let's start with the story of a pastor who arrived in town promising to fulfill all the desires of a struggling church long in need of a permanent pastor. The people of the church, among whom were many professionals, rejoiced that their search was finally over.

During a meeting with the church's core group, this new pastor promised to stay for a year and conveyed a willingness to leave if things did not work out. Once his job became official, however, it only took him a few months to run the church credit card balance up to six thousand dollars. He spent money extravagantly on multiple items for himself and for the church.

After a year, the church was in severe debt. One of the leaders who had originally invited this pastor to town took him to lunch and brought up his promise about reexamining things after the first year. The pastor replied defensively, "You don't have that in writing." Like many abusive leaders, he was unconcerned about increasing God's Kingdom. His own financial security was his first priority.

The downward spiral of the church continued. A member who had already resigned the board in disgust received an unexpected phone call from the bank, asking him what the church was going to do about the mortgage. The banker informed him that the church had not paid a note in six months. Appalled, the member recognized that the church could bring disgrace on the Kingdom of God in that city, so he called the pastor. Instead of facing reality about the church's finances, the pastor blatantly accused this former board member of bitterness and unforgiveness toward him. Typical of Jezebel controllers, the pastor sidetracked the real issue and shifted the blame to his confronter.

The mortgage was never paid, and the bank reluctantly repossessed the church. The building stood empty, but of course this pastor did not take responsibility—everything was someone else's fault. When he could extract no more money from the church, he resigned. Now he has a traveling ministry. Naturally, he does not bother to tell anyone about the irreparable damage he caused in that church and community. As he travels about, he only mentions that he served as a successful pastor.

This abusive leader was building his own kingdom and quality of life, not God's Kingdom. Yet in his eyes, he has excused himself from all wrongdoing. We will not know until eternity the amount of damage and loss he caused the Kingdom of God.

Known by Their Fruits

In another part of the United States, a man in his mid-thirties was invited to pastor a church where the previous pastor had retired. As I interviewed the board members long after the events I am about to relate, they informed me that he was a controller from the beginning. The first thing they noticed was that on his arrival, he did not come to the welcoming reception that was held for him. He was in town but just did not show up, nor did he apologize or explain why.

This inconsiderate pattern continued over his two-year stint. He never arrived on time at the weekly men's prayer meetings, sometimes not even showing up at all. The men would have to stand out in the parking lot and wait for him to come unlock the church. Often, they waited to no avail and then returned home. Again, no apologies or explanations were forthcoming. Also, the pastor frequently did not show up for midweek services, sending in an unannounced, unheard-of guest speaker instead. No one at the church ever knew for sure what was going on. This is a strong characteristic of Jezebel controllers—keeping you in the dark about their plans and using the element of surprise. This maintains their control.

This pastor also cunningly relocated his brother into the area and included him in decision making, putting him on staff at the church. The church members were irritated that his brother was edging his way in. He was not the one who had been hired, and it was unethical for him to share pastoral authority.

Then the pastor criticized the church's new organ, which the church had sacrificed to buy before he came. He demanded a new one but never got it. The music store where the organ had been purchased strongly advised against moving the organ around, yet this pastor had it moved weekly. Finally, he removed it from the auditorium, shoving it into a back storage room. He also began removing pictures from the walls because he did not like them. An artist in the church had painted several tasteful and professional scenes of Christ. They were removed with no regard for her feelings, and she was greatly hurt. When people are hurt or destroyed with no compassion or consideration for their feelings, something is missing. Even secular businesses show more consideration for the well-being of their employees.

Things became even stranger. This pastor callously told the congregation one Sunday that they had better get used to change. Then each week without exception, plants, chairs, furniture, musical instruments and so forth would be moved around or removed altogether. More and more he resorted to domination. After all, he had to show "authority."

This pastor also continually talked down his former church, elaborating about how he put in many extra hours and was never paid overtime. He complained about how the former church spent money, obviously angry that the money had not been spent solely on him. The board members at his new church greatly regretted that they had not asked for references before agreeing to hire him as their pastor.

Then money became the issue. He began writing church checks for everything and taking frequent "ministry" trips anywhere his heart desired. He rapidly depleted the church's twenty-thousand-dollar savings account. Checks began to bounce. The church board had to cover the bounced checks out of their own pockets over and over. The church's credit card debt went up into the thousands as the pastor spent money like water, taking his wife out for fancy dinners and making numerous other personal but "ministry-excused" purchases.

Worst of all, there was no flow of the Holy Spirit, only hype. The church had a history of glorious worship, but this pastor put a stop to that, bringing in a stuffy, manipulation-ridden form of music. Songs in the Spirit were replaced by fleshly shouting and loud, nerve-racking music.

Another of the pastor's relatives moved into the area and was hired to run the sound system. Large sums of money were spent on this relative, although previously the sound system had been capably run by church volunteers. People began to complain that the pastor had no conscience or integrity. Attendance quickly faded.

The church board confronted this pastor about his many improprieties and asked if he would consider resigning. He indicated that he was willing to leave, but he demanded enormous vacation pay, moving expenses and a large cash settlement. The board agreed to pay him, happy to be rid of him at any price. As one member put it, this pastor saw his position as purely a business venture anyway.

Although the board met all of his unreasonable requests, during the brief time that he remained, this pastor took a number of gullible people in the church to lunch and told them his distorted side of the story. Then he stood up on a Sunday morning and did a terrific job of sounding as though *he* were the victim, skillfully playing on people's emotions. He ended that service by saying he was turning the church over to the board, and he walked out the side door. Immediately, several families he had "prepared" (poisoned) stood up on cue and stomped out of the building. By the following week, the "fruit" of his ministry was even more evident. Only seven members remained in the church. The good news is that later a pastor with integrity and a pure heart was hired, and today the church is thriving.

His People, Not God's People

I was invited to minister to a church on a special holiday. The pastor invited another congregation from a town about one hundred miles away to join us in the weekend of celebration. During my first session, I sensed a tremendous unresponsiveness from a number of people, which troubled me.

At the next session, the pastor from the other town had a turn to preach. When he got up, the same people who had been so unresponsive almost revered him. He was their pastor, and I sensed that in their eyes he could do no wrong. It was obvious that he kept them captive with an inflated impression of his abilities. He projected himself as a scholar of the Word and made innuendos suggesting that all other Bible teachers knew nothing. There was no edification in my spirit from his preaching, which consisted of high-sounding phrases with no substance. After an hour, I could not write down one significant thing he said. Yet his people ate it up, and I had the feeling that he had so subdued them that in their eyes, he was more than perfect. They were *his* people, not God's people.

Looking back, I recognize now that this man was a Jezebel controller, not a man of God with a pastor's heart. To maintain a following, he had to project a sense of awe about himself, and he did it very well. The people were nearly glassy-eyed whenever he opened his mouth to say something. When he prophesied, the words were so grandiose that there was no sense of reality.

Nearly a year later, a minister friend of mine whom I had known for years approached this same pastor with a dilemma. My friend had had a minor moral failure and sought him out for counsel. My friend was extremely remorseful and wanted to do the right thing. This pastor "counseled" him to bring the situation before the entire church, relate every detail and then turn the church over to the elders, totally resigning his ministry. Before my friend followed this course of action, he called me and explained the situation. Although he was willing to submit, he did not feel he had received correct counsel.

I agreed. The counsel was from the man's head, not from the Spirit of God. Without compassion or concern, he mechanically told my friend to get out of the ministry and expose his sin to the entire church (which meant the entire community). It would have been one thing if my friend was habitual and unrepentant, but he was not. He was extremely remorseful. As I prayed with him, I felt that the mind of the Lord was that he was to handle the situation with as few people as possible by repenting to those involved (see Matthew 18:15–17). He followed my counsel and walked in righteousness, grateful for the grace and mercy of God. No one in his church or city got involved, and many lives were spared the hurt that a public confession would have caused. Years later, he is still walking with God and has an impeccable reputation. God has truly blessed him.

Clearly, this other pastor had no real compassion for my friend and desired to see him lose his ministry. After all, if my friend's ministry went down, that would make this controlling pastor's "unfailed" ministry look all the better. Where was love in his counsel? Love covers a multitude of sins. All he wanted to do was expose a sincerely repentant man who was supposed to be a friend. Later, this ego-ridden pastor who had wanted to see my friend exposed "lost it" and broke all his church's windows in an explosion of temper. The entire community saw who he really was.

Jezebel spirits are always hard and judgmental, mainly because it gives them a greater sense of control—"You failed and I didn't." But where is the Spirit of Christ? Where is love in that? I do not condone sin in any way. If someone is habitual and unrepentant in his sin, he should be exposed: "Have no fellowship with the unfruitful works of darkness, but rather expose them" (Ephesians 5:11). But when someone truly repents and seeks to make things right, why expose him? Why draw the entire Body of Christ into a situation that will help no one and hurt many innocent people? Why not extend mercy and cover the person with love? Galatians 6:1 tells us, "Brethren, if a man is overtaken in any trespass, you who are spiritual restore such a one in a spirit of gentleness, considering yourself lest you also be tempted."

Abuse of Young Associates

A young couple was hired as associate pastors of an established church. I was impressed with their pure hearts and teachable spirits. However, the senior pastor made unbelievable demands on them, insisting that they work long hours and never miss a board meeting. During this time they had a premature baby, born at barely over a pound. This baby girl was hospitalized off and on for four months and was in a life-threatening situation on several occasions. When the young father asked for an occasional partial day off during this time, the pastor defiantly denied his request and demanded he be at routine staff meetings instead. The pastor also refused to change the time of the meetings, even though the young associate's daughter was getting ready to undergo traumatic surgery.

When the baby was a month old, the hospital called requesting that these young parents come in immediately. Their daughter had contracted a yeast infection and was not expected to live. Our friends asked permission to leave after the worship portion of a service to make the one-hour drive to the hospital. They were told, "Absolutely not." The pastor insisted they be in the entire church service. The husband and wife conferred and made the decision to leave anyway because the situation involved their baby's life. The pastor finally conceded, telling them, "Go if you feel you *have* to . . . but be back tonight!" My friends were allowed only one day off during that four-month period, when the baby was at an extremely critical stage.

Over the duration of the baby's hospitalization, the pastor himself only visited the hospital twice. Both times, his visits were disastrous. It was a research hospital, and only relatives were allowed to visit at any length. When hospital staff informed him of their brief-visit regulations, he began loudly threatening the nurses, saying he would go to the hospital's top authorities. His young associates cringed at their pastor's offensiveness. They had tried to witness about the Lord to these nurses, but his inappropriate behavior left a huge black mark on the ministry, and they were terribly embarrassed. He also stayed far beyond the allowed time frame (even for a relative) and demanded detailed information from the nurses, who were appalled at his behavior. The nurses and these young parents quickly agreed that if the pastor came to the hospital again, he was not to be allowed in under any circumstances.

This young couple was also in charge of music for the church, and their pastor continually made unreasonable demands for productions and ruled with an iron hand regarding what songs to sing in church services. Time and time again, as they sought the Holy Spirit concerning songs and the flow of the worship service, this arrogant pastor overruled them. He also repeatedly took credit for many things this couple did behind the scenes to benefit the church. He did not mind letting people think he was responsible for the hard work his associates had done.

Because these associates were so pure before the Lord and had servant hearts, they endured this pastor's abuse for two years. Finally, something happened that forced them into a confrontation with him. A brother-in-law told the young man about a talk this pastor/employer had given at a pastors' conference the previous year, in which he had used the young associate and his wife as an example of certain types of personality defects. Appalled, the couple sought me out for counsel. I encouraged them to confront the pastor.

The following day, the associate called his pastor and confronted him about the message. The pastor confessed that he had indeed used them as an example in his talk. Having lost all respect for the man, the young associate indicated that he and his wife would like to resign immediately. A meeting was set up. This young couple did not want the church damaged, so for the sake of the church and its people, they desired a smooth and peaceful transition out.

Obviously, the pastor wanted to meet for a different reason. He feared a lawsuit for slander. That same evening, when the young associates were in their pajamas ready for bed, there was a knock on the door. To their amazement it was their pastor, accompanied by a pastor from a neighboring church. Although they had previously set up the meeting for the next morning, their pastor performed a typical Jezebel maneuver—he purposely caught them off guard. Using the element of surprise gave him the upper hand. Unprepared, the couple's defenses were weakened.

As the young associate and his wife stood there in their bath-robes, the two pastors invited themselves in and insisted they have an on-the-spot meeting. The couple reluctantly agreed, and the meeting was "conducted" right then and there. Because they were caught off guard and were totally unprepared with the things they had intended to bring to light, they simply agreed to resign and not press charges for the pastor's slanderous words.

These young associates had no intention of bringing a lawsuit anyway, although they were entitled to because their character had been maligned. They simply desired a meeting to clear the air and to state their case, citing the abuses of the past two years. But that pastor's Jezebel spirit reigned again, through the element of surprise. To the dismay of an entire congregation of people who loved them, the young associates resigned their position. In the process, they chose to protect the reputation of the church rather than dragging the matter out in front of everyone. When this couple's home was sold, one hundred people came from the church for a farewell party. The pastor did not come. Later, when the associate was happily attending a church in another state, this pastor called his new pastor and maligned him once again. It was not received.

One of the comments this pastor flippantly made at the surprise meeting was that the secular world never would have given the young associates time off for anything. However, the young man began working for a wonderful company in another state, and in just a few months, he was promoted to a prominent position that would usually take a decade to reach. God vindicated his excellent character. His new employer compassionately informed him that any time an immediate family member was in the hospital, it was the company's policy to give as much time off as is needed (with pay). A few years later, the Lord opened the door for my friends to become senior pastors of a church in another state, where they are blessed beyond measure.

The future did not go as smoothly for their former controlling pastor. Thank God the true fruit of his ministry was revealed, because within a year his entire new staff resigned, unable to work with him. God separates the sheep from the goats.

No God-Given Authority

A close friend of mine attended a church where the pastor was so insecure that seemingly he had no God-given authority. He relied totally on projecting himself as an authority figure. He commonly referred to himself as the door of "his" church and continually reminded the people that no one had the right to question his authority.

My friend, a member at this church for many years, did his best to take on the heart of a servant. Most people recognized our friend as seasoned and he had a close walk with God, but his pastor never invited him to do anything involving leadership. On one occasion, they were together at a meeting and the Lord strongly anointed my friend to minister to a visiting pastor with a great need. The way he ministered was very prophetic, and he was obviously under a heavy anointing. When he finished ministering, his pastor stood up, grabbed the microphone and began to brag on him in front of the group in such a way that he was clearly saying, "I'm responsible for this man's spiritual level."

Typical of someone with a Jezebel spirit, this pastor quickly credited himself for anything positive and also would quickly separate himself from blame for anything. He also continually surrounded himself with "yes" men. He would seek out those with little or no backbone, Ahab types who would rarely question his decisions on anything.

During testimonial times, this pastor would rarely thank Jesus or exalt the Lord. As a rule, Jezebels can give God credit verbally but not from their hearts. They see themselves as in control, not God. They also need parade and show, and always have to be center stage.

Also typical of a Jezebel, this pastor was very competitive. Jezebels hate to lose and will not back down. Our friend shared with us that even in a Saturday afternoon basketball game, this pastor hated to lose and would express anger and total dissatisfaction over a loss. He was not in control if he lost!

My friend's pastor was very two-faced. He would strive to please both sides. Showing great favoritism, he worked hard to please everyone, but his motive was obvious—he wanted total control. He frequently used flattery to win people to himself, bragging about how good they were.

Toward the end of this pastor's tenure with this church, he became more and more rigid. He began to teach from the book of Revelation and would frequently comment, "I don't care what anyone says—I'm right." He had studied Revelation for several weeks, and who could possibly know more about the book than he did? He began to seek out more education, pulling strings to take courses in nearby prestigious schools. He would then brag incessantly about attending those schools. It was obvious to even his closest church members that he was pursuing education out of insecurity and not the mind of the Spirit.

A great lack of humility seems to characterize all Jezebels. Controlling spirits work from a pivotal point of pride. Naturally, the pride is of a twisted sort, somehow birthed out of extreme inferiority and insecurity—but it is pride nevertheless.

A Know-It-All Pastor

Some friends of mine encountered another Jezebel pastor. This pastor proclaimed that God had called him to a certain city, and he became pastor of a church there. One veteran Christian turned over his long-time Friday-night youth Bible study to this pastor. Instead of teaching the teens and imparting godliness, however, the man got the youth involved in "Christian" rock music. Within six months, the teens were all gone, either back in the world or turned off to the things of the Lord.

This pastor also caused a great deal of alarm when he emphasized deliverance meetings for the young people. Each session ended with the youth screaming violently on the floor. This filled many with fear, and it was no surprise that people soon stopped coming to the church. It takes little delving into Scripture to note that Jesus *always* told the demons to be quiet. However, this pastor's ego needed to see the young people screaming (equating this "manifestation" with spiritual results), even though absolutely no fruit ever came of the display.

Things finally came to a head when the church attempted to buy a building. This pastor tried to finagle the bank financing to include the purchase of his own home. At a board meeting, he demanded that each elder cosign for a huge loan for a church building—a loan that included his two-hundred-thousand-dollar home. One by one, concerned board members spoke up, saying that they just could not jeopardize their own financial security that way. In response, this pastor stomped out of the office. Manipulation was one of his most effectual tools; he loaded guilt on anyone who would not embrace his selfish plans.

A successful Realtor in the church tried to explain to this pastor (in vain) how the church was financially unable to take on this enormous endeavor. He rejected the Realtor's counsel. He also rejected a Christian attorney's counsel. He would only receive input that corresponded with what he had already planned to do. Those who disagreed with his actions had to endure sermons he conspicuously preached against them, including remarks such as, "There are some who won't back the pastor." Ultimately, he successfully alienated every bank in the city, berating them when they would not grant him the loan he wanted.

This pastor always complained about the young church's lack of finances, yet nearly every day he freely used church funds to buy himself and his friends expensive lunches. He also purchased five new cars in his two years as pastor. While the faithful congregants were struggling to keep the church afloat, he spent the church's money freely on various gadgets for himself. He was rarely in town, always off at a vitamin convention, on a hunting trip or involved in some other personal endeavor. Rarely was he at home more than two weeks a month.

A guest evangelist who came to minister at the church warned this pastor publicly about two things. He said, "Do not get into debt," and "Watch your pride." The pastor ignored those warnings and deliberately took the church into enormous debt, refusing to submit his ego to God.

The fruit of his ministry was that the entire church disbanded. This pastor is off in another city, repeating the same scenario at another church. His former church members tried to warn the leaders to whom he had freshly "submitted" himself. However, the new group was too excited about his being a part of their organization to listen. They will learn about his Jezebel spirit the hard way. It is hard to imagine how many souls will be eternally wounded in the process. Maybe someday this abusive "leader" will be able to receive correction from God.

People Who Preferred Coercion

A friend of mine accepted the pastorate of a church with three hundred members. The church thrived under his preaching at first, until the Holy Spirit began to move against their tradition. The old wineskins had no tolerance or desire for anything fresh from the Spirit. As this anointed and gifted pastor tried to yield to the purposes of God, he found himself facing fierce opposition. Soon a rumor was started against him, and a committee formed to vote him out. The politicking was unbelievable, with people putting in their votes two and three times. One man even had his invalid mother, who had not been in church for a year, vote. Her mental condition prevented her from even knowing what she was doing.

Upon leaving, our friend spoke frankly to the church's committee concerning a man they were seeking to replace him. He said, "This man will do to you what you did to me." Soon after the new pastor was installed, he began to take from the church financially and caused great division. When he finally resigned from the church, which eventually saw through his tactics, real damage had been done. It reminds one of the warnings God gave Israel when they desired a king like other nations had:

> So Samuel told all the words of the LORD to the people who asked him for a king. And he said, "This will be the behavior of the king who will reign over you: He will take your sons and appoint them for his own chariots and to be his horsemen . . . He will take your daughters to be perfumers, cooks, and bakers. And he will take the best of your fields, your vineyards, and your olive groves, and give them to his servants. He will take a tenth of your grain and your vintage, and give it to his officers and servants. And he will take your male servants, your female servants, your finest young men, and your donkeys, and put them to his work. He will take a tenth of your sheep. And you will be his servants."
>
> 1 Samuel 8:10–17

The new pastor went from house to house, taking people aside, picking those naïve enough to somehow believe that the church had ripped him off. He gained sympathy until he had a favorable following. The same people who would not stand with our friend for legitimate reasons now stood with this new man who was functioning totally under a Jezebel spirit.

A year previously, my friend had moved to another town and started a new work from scratch. The people who had claimed loyalty but did not stand with him when he was persecuted now followed this recently expelled Jezebel pastor. Where do you suppose the man started a church? In the same town as our friend! He blatantly began to compete with him there. Again, it seems that people would rather be coerced than led. Our friend had the pure motive of starting a church that could experience pure worship with the Holy Spirit in control. Although his former church people saw it, they were not strong enough to shake their denominational ties. Our friend had tried to lead them in the way of the Spirit, but they would not go. Yet now they had become extremely loyal to a Jezebel. When the Jezebel coerced them, they followed him. Now, three years later, those once so appreciative of our friend's message have never darkened the door of his new church.

This story becomes more incredible. The Jezebel pastor continually sows bad seed against my friend. When my friend has a guest minister in, this pastor finds out the dates and invites a guest in for the very same dates. Our friend had a tremendously successful tent meeting his first summer in the new town. The next year he planned it again. To his amazement, this Jezebel pastor also planned a tent meeting during the same dates. The third year, the man again planned a tent meeting on the same dates as our friend, although the dates were set a year in advance and he could have chosen another time.

Insecurity runs rampant in this Jezebel pastor! Extremely possessive of his people, he cannot bear to let his competition with our friend go, for fear of losing his people. His coerced people continue to believe every lie and follow him loyally.

Like Old Testament Israel, some people today would rather be coerced than led. God wants to lead His people personally. When will we learn? Apparently, some would still rather have man tell them a lie than take the trouble to go to God for the truth. The wonderful truth of the New Covenant is that we can all know the Lord personally and individually. "None of them shall teach his neighbor, and none his brother, saying, 'Know the Lord,' *for all shall know Me, from the least of them to the greatest of them*" (Hebrews 8:11, emphasis added).

All the leaders I have mentioned in these stories seem to have personal gain issues, an uncrucified ego, strong self-centeredness and a need to be recognized by people more than by God. In their quest for power, they seem to have no problem with inconsistencies, extravagance, lies and distortions. Truly, all these control issues open the door to the Jezebel principality, which finds access through the flesh.

Questions to Consider

1. Why is the ego such an affront to God?
2. How do those in leadership positions try to establish control?
3. Explain the difference between submitting to God's authority and submitting to ungodly authority.
4. How do fear and insecurity play a role in ungodly authority figures?

Prayer

Lord, help me serve You with humility and always have the heart of a servant. Forgive me for any wrong motives. Help me desire only to increase Your Kingdom, never my own. In Jesus' name, Amen.

11

What Can I Do about Jezebel?

Can people with a Jezebel spirit come to repentance? Yes, absolutely. First, however, they must recognize their behavioral patterns and controlling motives and ruthlessly be willing to face the truth. They must let God crucify their flesh. Then, to be permanently set free, they must subject the flesh and all its patterns to the Holy Spirit daily.

Freedom can come when someone who is not afraid of a reaction confronts a person who has a Jezebel spirit. Confronted in firmness and love, the person may recognize that spirit and its effects, and he or she may respond by repenting and seeking deliverance. As I said back in chapter 2, the only way to get rid of a Jezebel spirit is to bring truth to the one under deception. Truth always trumps deception. Without a confrontation with the truth, people under the influence of Jezebel have no motive to change and will continue in the controlling lifestyle that has been their pattern for so long.

Both deception and truth have the ability to take root in the human heart, thereby guiding our actions. Deception can be powerful and enticing. When a person—any person, believer or unbeliever—is unwilling to search out and embrace the truth, he or she will always be bound by deception. But when deception is brought into the light, the enemy's lies are revealed. God's Word brings revelation and freedom. The light of the Word illuminated in the human heart is what casts out darkness. As Jesus said, "You shall know the truth, and the truth shall make you free" (John 8:32).

Am I the One?

Perhaps instead of facing another person who has a Jezebel spirit, you are facing yourself and have noticed some controlling tendencies that raise warning flags in you. After reading the stories in this book and thinking about the behavioral traits we have listed, you may see yourself in some of these pages and be asking, *Am I the one influenced by this spirit? How can I be free of Jezebel?* These are important questions to start with on the road to repentance. It is good for you as a believer to ask yourself some hard questions. They can be a tremendous step toward liberation from a controlling way of life.

If you are wondering whether you have opened yourself up to the influence of Jezebel, here are some other questions to carefully consider:

1. Have you ever taken part in forcing a pastor out of his position?
2. Are you jealous of other people by nature?
3. Have you ever slandered someone to make yourself look good?
4. Have you ever manipulated others by putting guilt on them? Have you ever used anger or tears to get others to do something you want?

5. Have you found yourself in constant conflict with authority throughout your life? For example, when you have changed churches or jobs, have you left thinking, *That person was the worst pastor (or worst boss) ever?*
6. Have you allowed yourself to feel resentful toward people who hold a position of leadership or authority?
7. Have you ever tried to get rid of someone else in order to set yourself up?

These sins do not mean that you are a Jezebel, yet if you have taken part in them or others like them, you may be manifesting some of Jezebel's characteristics. They are a fruit of the flesh, and you need to get them out of the way in order to go on in your spiritual life and avoid the judgment such sin always brings.

Repentance Brings Freedom

How do you get Jezebel's influence and characteristics out of your life? There is nothing like true repentance to render a spirit of Jezebel inoperative! Repentance brings freedom. Praying Psalm 51 for a period of time can be very beneficial and powerful. Ask the Lord to help you focus on specific verses and areas of your life in which you need to repent and change—verses like "Create in me a clean heart, O God, and renew a steadfast spirit within me" (verse 10).

"Though the LORD is on high, yet He regards the lowly; but the proud He knows from afar" (Psalm 138:6). From His high and lofty position, the Lord observes every heart. He is not looking for the boastful and arrogant, but for the humble and contrite. Although He is Creator of all the universe, He is looking for the spiritually bankrupt whose hearts are crushed. "On this one will I look: on him who is poor and of a contrite spirit, and who trembles at My word" (Isaiah 66:2).

The key characteristic of the humble and contrite is that they respond with reverence when they hear God's Word. What does the Lord desire to do with them? He wants to bring spiritual restoration: "Though I walk in the midst of trouble, You will revive me" (Psalm 138:7). The God of compassion wants to restore the crushed. "The LORD is near to those who have a broken heart, and saves such as have a contrite spirit" (Psalm 43:18). "He heals the brokenhearted and binds up their wounds" (Psalm 147:3). "He raises the poor out of the dust, and lifts the needy out of the ash heap" (Psalm 113:7).

Even if you have opened the door to a Jezebel spirit in the past, you can close the door now and be free—if you are determined to walk in true repentance and to change. No matter where you are spiritually, these truths are the beginning of your restoration.

Disdain for Jezebel

When believers surrender totally to the person and nature of Christ, it terrifies and cripples the power of darkness more than anything else. To be Christlike is to wield a powerful weapon against the enemy, because, after all, Satan and the Jezebel principality are specifically opposed to the nature of Christ.

To have a disdain and intolerance for all types of Jezebel's influence, there must be consistency in our lives as believers. We must pursue the Lord until there are no grounds on which the enemy can point a finger at us (see John 14:30). For example, many times we who rejoice and worship the Lord in church come home later and watch immoral entertainment on television. When we tolerate Jezebel's influence in our private lives, we give it inroads into the sanctuary of our lives. Our inconsistent behavior does not fool God. As Revelation 2:20 says, "Nevertheless, I have a few things against you, because you allow that woman Jezebel, who calls herself a prophetess, to teach and to seduce My servants to commit sexual immorality, and eat things sacrificed to idols."

By tolerating Jezebel, we greatly hinder the flow of God's power in our lives and our effectiveness for Him. The strategy of the devil is not just to tempt us to sin, but to bring us into shame so that we become emasculated and weakened in our authority to resist him. The bottom line is that we must equip ourselves with new resolve to war against Jezebel. Rather than sulking in condemnation over sins we have so easily given in to, we need to war aggressively against Jezebel and shake off all its influence.

Next to being Christlike, there is nothing in us that a Jezebel spirit fears more than prayer. Real prayer is simply praying what is on the mind of God. Strategic prayer is coming into alignment with God's thoughts and praying specifically therein. Many are bound to praying their own agenda. There is no power in that. True intercessory prayer is praying God's agenda. That kind of prayer throws a wrecking ball on the strategies of Jezebel and extracts its influence from the souls of men.

Intercessory prayer turns people's hearts away from immorality, bringing true repentance and godliness. True, fervent prayer causes hearts to change from pride and loftiness to repentance and humility. Nothing brings a greater death blow to the principality of Jezebel and its host of fallen spirits. Pray according to God's Word. Jezebel no doubt fears most the spoken Word of God as it comes forth with creative power.

Walking in Victory

What can you and I do about Jezebel? How can we walk in victory over this principality and its evil spirits, which infiltrate any open doors people provide in the weakness of their flesh? In chapter 6, I listed the important steps pastors and other leaders can take in dealing with a person who has a Jezebel spirit. And just above, I listed the questions you can ask yourself if you feel you may be the one under Jezebel's influence. In addition, however, there are several things I believe *all* of us can do to walk in victory. I want to list here some mandatory steps you and I can take, both to confront this spirit of hell and to minimize its influence in our lives, in our families and in our churches. These steps will help protect us from coming under the grip of a Jezebel spirit and trying to control others. These steps will also help us avoid allowing someone already under the control of Jezebel to manipulate and abuse us.

1. Develop and strengthen your inner life. Our battle is not against flesh and blood, so time alone with God building up the inner man is foremost. Meditate on the truth, pray and learn to stand firm. Listen to the still, small voice of the Father. Get His wisdom!

2. Forgive and bless your parents and every authority figure who has wronged you. This step is major if you need healing from wounds of the past and protection from spiritual attack.

3. Seek the baptism in the Holy Spirit. This power is available to every Christian. It is unwise for any believer *not* to take advantage of this mighty gift of God in these evil days.

4. Seek inner healing and deliverance. Everyone has been wounded by life and subjected to demonic attacks and the formation of strongholds. To the degree that you experience true freedom through inner healing and deliverance from demons is the degree you will walk in victory over Jezebel.

5. Ask God to show you generational patterns and possible curses; then ask Him to break them. Patterns that were

modeled for you and curses passed down from another generation need not remain part of your life.

6. Understand and apply the power of the cross, which can deliver us from ourselves. The Lord Jesus crucified your selfishness and self-centeredness on the cross. Ask Him to reveal every area of your flesh that you have not reckoned dead, and submit those areas to Him (see Romans 6:12).

7. Be alert to the patterns of Jezebel in your life and in those around you. Ask God for discernment, and use righteousness judgment when you encounter people controlled by a Jezebel spirit—make sure you deal with your own issues first, not being a forgetful hearer, but rather a doer of the Word (see James 1:25).

8. If you have been in the grip of Jezebel, expect warfare as you seek deliverance into a new walk. This spirit wants to destroy you. Your daily battle for freedom may not involve "knockout" capabilities, but rather inch-by-inch, point-counterpoint progress. Patterns of behavior that have long been in development may not necessarily change overnight, but they *will* change as you submit yourself to Christ.

9. Forgive as quickly and as deeply as you can. Unforgiveness is an open door to the enemy!

10. Bless and do not curse; do not return evil for evil. You break curses by blessing, giving thanks in everything and knowing that God works everything for your good.

11. Daily lay down everything in your life at the feet of Jesus. As martyred missionary Jim Elliot said, "He is no fool who gives what he cannot keep to gain that which he cannot lose." *Only* what is spiritual will pass beyond the grave.

12. Use this book as a battle plan. I trust there are priceless nuggets here that will sharpen your sword and open your eyes.

13. Be keenly aware of how subtle Jezebel's seduction of your spirit, mind and body can be. Jezebel is crafty and can easily play on your senses and emotions.

14. Learn to walk in agape love. Worldly, carnal people—and many Christians—walk in eros, a selfish "What's in it for me?" kind of love. Ask God to teach you how to walk in, live in and breathe in His love working in and through you. You will never be the same!

You have just finished reading and contemplating a lot of information about the Jezebel principality and the spirits it works through. Waging war on Jezebel is a hugely important issue in these last days because Jezebel's tactics are increasing and its goals are nowhere near completion. As a matter of fact, the methods of our archenemies will grow bigger and more vicious as we approach the end, because Satan knows his time is short (see Revelation 12:12).

It is imperative, then, that every child of God be "wise as serpents and harmless as doves" (Matthew 10:16). If we are to walk in victory, there is no room in the Church for the aggression of a Jezebel or the passivity of an Ahab. We must live assertively, as Jesus did, and walk in the presence and power of the Holy Spirit as we discern and deal with this already defeated foe.

Questions to Consider

1. When you examine your own behaviors, do you find anything that may have Jezebel's influence at its roots?

2. Why is a humble and contrite heart so important in freeing ourselves from Jezebel's control?

3. How does intercessory prayer wreck the strategies of Jezebel?

Prayer

In this book you have seen the many ways of a Jezebel. If you recognize any of these traits in your own life, pray this prayer:

Father, I acknowledge that I have yielded myself to a spirit of Jezebel. I come to You, humbling myself before You. I desire Your standard of righteousness and holiness. I ask You to forgive me for my tolerance of the Jezebel spirit and for being sympathetic to its ways. Please forgive me for every way I have opened myself to this spirit. Help me ruthlessly reject every type of thinking related to the desire to control and manipulate others. I renounce and bind this demon of Jezebel, and I pull down this stronghold in my life. Through the Holy Spirit, I will live by Your standard of righteousness, holiness and conduct. Open my eyes and cause Your light to expose any darkness, and help me walk in humility and truth. In Jesus' name, Amen.

If you have seen the influence of either Jezebel or Ahab spirits in those around you, whether in your church, your workplace or at home, pray this prayer:

Lord, help me be discerning and compassionate, yet firm, as I assertively challenge the enemies of Your cross. Help me never again to live with a tolerant attitude toward those activities that come out of the influence of Jezebel or Ahab spirits. Help me not to fear the consequences of confronting such behaviors, because I am more concerned about pleasing You. In Jesus' name, Amen.

Steve Sampson is a gifted writer and effective minister who provides the Body of Christ with thought-provoking insights about the ministry of the Holy Spirit. Characterized as a Christian Bob Newhart, his unique wit combines candor and transparency, while refreshing the soul of the hearer.

Through the prophetic gifts of the Holy Spirit, Steve has ministered to people for decades by speaking personal vision, hope and expectation into their lives. Demonstrating how the Holy Spirit speaks to people, he has been a source of encouragement for others who seek to experience the power and fullness of life in the Spirit.

You can contact Steve about ministry events and available teaching resources at:

Steve Sampson Ministries
P.O. Box 36324
Birmingham, AL 35236
www.stevesampson.com